The New York Times

COZY CROSSWORDS
75 Light and Easy Puzzles

Edited by Will Shortz

ST. MARTIN'S GRIFFIN ✄ NEW YORK

The New York Times

COZY CROSSWORDS

ACROSS

1 Listings in a dr.'s calendar
6 Number of Muses
10 Best guesses: Abbr.
14 Nary ___ (no one)
15 Grandson of Adam
16 March Madness org.
17 Parting words from the Everly Brothers
19 Unrestrained revelry
20 "Clean up your ___!"
21 "___ Baba and the 40 Thieves"
22 "___ me, Father" (confessional phrase)
23 Parting words from the Lone Ranger
28 Card game for two
29 "Telephone Line" rock group
30 Diminutive suffix
31 ___-Coburg-Gotha, former British royal house
32 Heavenly body
33 Gorillas
34 Parting words from the Terminator
38 Degs. for corporate types
41 ___ Lingus
42 Hula dancers wiggle them
45 Building wing
46 Suffix with labyrinth
47 Reply to "Am not!"
49 Parting words from the von Trapps
52 Laughs
53 Forbid
54 Bowling stat.
56 Western Indian tribe
57 Parting words from Donald Trump
61 Halliwell of the Spice Girls
62 Claudia ___ Taylor (Lady Bird Johnson)
63 Director Kurosawa
64 Fruity drinks
65 Dennis the Menace, for one
66 Not tidy

DOWN

1 Four-line rhyme scheme
2 Human spirits
3 Horace's "Ars ___"
4 Bath site
5 Foxy
6 Nervous ___
7 How French fries are fried
8 Oct. follower
9 Language suffix
10 W.W. II bomber ___ Gay
11 Homer Simpson type
12 Common house event before moving
13 Agrees
18 Sunrise direction
22 Pal
24 Vertical line on a graph
25 Hershiser on the mound
26 Subject follower
27 Isle of exile
32 "___ the ramparts . . ."
33 "Go fly ___!"
35 Fritz who directed "Metropolis"
36 Hamburger meat
37 "___ your food" (mother's admonition)
38 Yiddish for "crazy"
39 Like a stomach after an all-you-can-eat buffet
40 Fully focused and attentive
43 North Star
44 Crossword doers
46 ___ and outs
47 Mount where Noah landed
48 Artist Magritte
50 Place for camels to water
51 Touches
55 "Hello" Down Under
57 Talk noisily
58 Bullfight cheer
59 Clan: Abbr.
60 '50s prez

by Jay Kaskel

2

ACROSS

1 You might fix one yourself at a bar
6 Abbr. after a lawyer's name
9 Blog additions
14 Dance partner for Fred
15 Little, in Lille
16 "99 and 44/100% pure" soap
17 Place for knickknacks
18 "What ___ to do?"
19 Link
20 Thief in a western
23 Rm. coolers
24 ___-de-sac
25 Suffix with Orwell
26 Bard's "before"
29 Some metal frames
32 "Dancing Queen" group
35 Penn, e.g.: Abbr.
36 They're red or blue, on some maps
37 Emergency strategy
39 N.L. cap letters
41 "All About ___," 2009 Sandra Bullock bomb
42 Main lines
44 Canon camera line
46 "___ Tu" (1974 hit)
47 Parliamentary procedure guide, familiarly
50 Outcomes of some QB sneaks
51 Bacon runoff
52 Suffix with penta-
53 ___ few rounds (spar)
56 Unclear outcome . . . or what can be found literally in 20-, 29- and 47-Across
59 Hip-hopper's headgear
62 Battery for many penlights
63 Modular elements
64 PayPal money, e.g.
65 Chain part: Abbr.
66 Little Munster
67 SALT subject
68 To date
69 Accomplish, biblically

DOWN

1 The younger Obama girl
2 Specially formed, as a committee
3 Lascivious looks
4 Tell-___ (some bios)
5 Reason for a merchandise return
6 Adornments on officers' shoulders
7 Coll. terms
8 "Knock that off!"
9 Pesto ingredients
10 In the strike zone
11 Beantown or Chi-Town team
12 Play about Capote
13 Part of CBS: Abbr.
21 They intersect in Montréal
22 TV husband of Phyllis
26 Perfumery compound
27 Christopher of "Somewhere in Time"
28 Slalom paths
29 "À votre ___!"
30 "I'm outta here!"
31 Fills to the gills
32 In pieces
33 Red Cross supply
34 Verbal digs
38 A bouncer might break one up
40 TV boss of Mary Richards
43 Record label for Booker T. & the M.G.'s
45 Gin flavoring
48 Like a Turkish bath
49 Came next
53 Go like a flying squirrel
54 Super Bowl XXV M.V.P. ___ Anderson
55 Item in the plus column
56 Communion service
57 See socially
58 "Go back," on an edit menu
59 TV room
60 World Food Day mo.
61 "Norma ___"

by Peter A. Collins

3

ACROSS

1 Intimidate
6 Group of eight
11 Jazz style
14 Mary of "The Maltese Falcon," 1941
15 Rose ___, group with the 1977 #1 hit "Car Wash"
16 Bibliophile's suffix
17 2010 Guinness world record at 1,689 lbs.
20 "Well, ___-di-dah!"
21 Cybermemo
22 Put up
23 Yoga posture
24 Stockbrokers' orders
25 1975 Pulitzer-winning critic
28 Successor to Frist as Senate majority leader
29 2010 Guinness world record at 11 ft. 6 in.
36 Director Lee
37 Time on end
38 Shake a leg
39 2010 Guinness world record at 72 lbs. 9 oz.
44 Court legend
45 Stirs up
46 Mario Puzo best seller
49 Actor Lloyd
52 Restaurant reading
53 Yard menaces
54 Staff's partner
57 2010 Guinness world record at 115 ft.
60 Roxy Music co-founder
61 Mr. who squints
62 Stand out
63 Part of A.A.R.P.: Abbr.
64 A whole bunch
65 "Navy Blue" singer Renay

DOWN

1 Willy Wonka's creator
2 Where whalers go
3 Home of the city Bountiful
4 Topaz mo.
5 Adriatic port
6 Director Welles
7 Terra ___
8 Font contents
9 Prefix with puncture
10 Class clown's "reward," often
11 Lay in the hot sun
12 Standing by
13 What suspenders suspend
18 Disney deer
19 Gucci rival
23 1978 World Cup winner: Abbr.
24 "The Gondoliers" girl
25 Mideast carrier
26 ___ fides
27 Mech. expert
28 Mysterious character
30 "I Am . . . ___ Fierce," #1 Beyoncé album
31 Place for un béret
32 May honoree
33 Indian spiced tea
34 Challenge for Jack and Jill
35 Snaky swimmers
40 Country crooner Brooks
41 Values
42 Seriously bad-mouthed
43 "___ appétit!"
46 Orangish yellow
47 Northern terminus of U.S. 1
48 Grain disease
49 At all, in dialect
50 Mishmashes
51 Part of an itinerary
53 Homeowner's debt: Abbr.
54 Costa ___
55 It's often operated with a dial
56 Strike out
58 Erie Canal mule
59 511, to Caesar

by Robert A. Doll

4

ACROSS

1 Cow's offspring
5 U.C.L.A. player
10 Bank no.
14 Margarine
15 Copy, for short
16 What's seen in "Saw"
17 Football alignment named for its shape
19 "___ a Song Go Out of My Heart"
20 Impertinent
21 Bed-and-breakfast
22 Muslim's God
23 Elvis ___ Presley
25 Drug that's a downer
26 Top choice
31 Sign in a boardinghouse window
32 "Yes, captain!"
33 Good "Wheel of Fortune" purchase for STRING BIKINI
34 Drano ingredient
35 Undeveloped
38 Heckle or Jeckle of cartoons
42 Lay waste to
45 "Light" dessert?
48 Went nuts
49 School near Windsor Castle
50 11th-century conqueror of Valencia
51 Number on a golf hole
53 Starbucks size that's Italian for "twenty"
57 Fruity drinks
58 Sci-fi hero in the 25th century
60 Circus shelter
61 Stan's pal in old films
62 Puccini's "Nessun dorma," for one
63 Captain Hook's henchman
64 To the point, ironically
65 Classic theater name

DOWN

1 Foldable beds
2 ___ Romeo (Italian car)
3 Ones born before Virgos
4 Abandon
5 Item under a blouse
6 Color again, as the hair
7 Go ___ smoke
8 Do a post-washing chore
9 Oui's opposite
10 Nimbleness
11 Property securing a loan
12 Manufacture
13 Restraining cord
18 Ancient Athenian sculptor
22 Samoan capital
24 Frequent, in poetry
25 Cheer for a bullfighter
26 School org.
27 Charged particle
28 It might be marked off with police tape
29 Rutherford B. ___
30 Ogle
34 Big fib
36 Biographical datum
37 Itsy-bitsy
39 Skilled entertainer
40 Where to enter this puzzle's answers
41 Indy 500 service area
42 Same old same old
43 From the beginning: Lat.
44 The "sour" in sweet-and-sour
45 Shoe grippers
46 Poker variety
47 Sleeveless jacket
51 Word on a door handle
52 Org. protecting individual rights
54 Literary Wolfe
55 "___ are for kids" (ad slogan)
56 "___, old chap!"
58 Go up and down, as in the water
59 On Social Security: Abbr.

by Bob Johnson

ACROSS

1 Deep-six
5 Crosswise, on deck
10 Movie lot sights
14 "Beat it!"
15 Martini's partner in wine
16 Turkish title of old
17 Not stuffy
18 Pesky swarm
19 H.S. math class
20 Keypad forerunner
22 Safecracker
23 They, in Thiers
24 Coarse, as humor
26 Knock down in rank
30 Term of address from a hat-tipper
32 Seat of Marion County, Fla.
33 Ghana, once
38 Company that makes Lincoln and Mercury
39 Afternoon fare . . . or a hint to the ends of 20-, 33-, 41- and 52-Across
40 Eliciting a "So what?"
41 Body suit shade, perhaps
43 Community of plant and animal life
44 Blossoms-to-be
45 Glossy fabric
46 Absolutely perfect
50 Mineo of "Exodus"
51 Zap in the microwave
52 One of two in a Christmas song
59 "Axis of evil" land
60 Stiller's partner in comedy
61 Like thrift shop wares
62 Snowman's prop
63 Vows locale

64 Came into a base horizontally
65 Give off
66 Down and out
67 Broadway honor

DOWN

1 Peter the Great, e.g.
2 Kent State locale
3 Do a laundry chore
4 __ beans (miso ingredients)
5 Pattern named for a Scottish county
6 Wall Street buys
7 Morales of "La Bamba"
8 Terrier in whodunits
9 Isn't completely honest with
10 Lecherous figure of Greek myth
11 Everglades wader
12 Chicken piece
13 Drooping
21 Meter maid of song
25 Onetime Jeep mfr.
26 Tip, as a hat
27 Earth Day subj.
28 Foal's mother
29 Cutlass or 88
30 Haunted house sounds
31 Mont Blanc, par exemple
33 Well-behaved
34 Article that may list survivors, in brief
35 Burn soother
36 Common bar order, with "the"
37 "That was __ . . ."
39 Movie double, often

42 "Def Comedy Jam" channel
43 Seat at a barn dance
45 Job interview topic
46 Take potshots (at)
47 Jewish holiday when the book of Esther is read
48 Cousin of a giraffe
49 Basic belief
50 Fine fiddle, for short
53 River to the Ubangi
54 Credit card statement figure
55 Do some housecleaning
56 Capital on a fjord
57 Way to a man's heart?
58 Whirling water

by Sarah Keller

6

ACROSS

1 Ninny
5 Actor Danny of "The Color Purple"
11 Jungle menace
14 "___ 911!" (former Comedy Central show)
15 Dub over
16 English novelist Radcliffe
17 Abbr. before a name in a memo
18 Promptly
19 Like zinfandel wines
20 Chokes after bean eating?
23 No room at the ___
24 The Engineers of the N.C.A.A.: Abbr.
25 Not all
27 Gave up
29 Monk's karate blows?
34 Business card abbr.
36 Shade of blue
37 When clocks are set ahead: Abbr.
38 Movie finales featuring actress Miles?
41 ___ Lanka
43 In ___ of
44 Fr. holy woman
45 Result of a sweetener overload?
48 Wife of Hägar the Horrible
52 Tints
53 China's Chou En-___
55 Metalliferous rock
56 Modern educational phenomenon . . . or a hint to 20-, 29-, 38- and 45-Across

62 The Windy City, briefly
63 Fearsome wooden roller coaster at Six Flags Great Adventure
64 Plains Indian
65 Cool, man
66 Nearing midnight
67 Johnston in 2008–09 news
68 Broke a fast
69 Newly fashioned
70 Harriet Beecher Stowe novel

DOWN

1 Like some irony
2 Sloppy kiss
3 Mean
4 Lots and lots
5 Congregation
6 Soup bean
7 Not duped by
8 Futile
9 Novel on which "Clueless" is based
10 Recite rapidly, with "off"
11 Peevish states
12 Interstate entrances
13 "Pick a number, ___ number"
21 Hospital attendant
22 Noncommittal suffix
26 Approx. number
28 Time off from l'école
30 Per ___
31 Magazine featuring 47-Down
32 Alamo competitor
33 "Sex and the City" actress Nixon
35 Not of the cloth
38 Like some tomatoes

39 Abbr. in help-wanted ads
40 Exclamation before "I didn't know that!"
41 Library admonishment
42 Camp in the wild
46 That, to Juanita
47 ___ E. Neuman
49 Hang around
50 Pronounced rhythm, in music
51 Origin of the phrase "Beware of Greeks bearing gifts"
54 Unassisted
57 ___ Xing
58 She, in Cherbourg
59 Twosome
60 ___ Scotia
61 Tattled
62 When doubled, a dance

by Anna Shechtman

ACROSS

1 Growing older
6 Tool for horses' hooves
10 Protective wear for lobster eaters
14 Region of ancient Asia Minor
15 "Hmm . . ."
16 Amo, amas, ___ . . .
17 Blue things that make some people turn red?
19 "Dear ___"
20 Sound systems
21 Actor/rapper ___ Def
23 Seedy loaf
24 Metal in a mountain
25 Nine-to-five gigs, often
27 Frequently, to Donne
30 Ran, as colors
32 "Othello" villain
33 Title for a prince or princess: Abbr.
34 Tennis's Nastase
35 As one
37 "___ the ramparts we watched . . ."
38 Womanizer
40 "___ Loser" (Beatles song)
41 Donkey's sound
43 "Give it ___!"
44 20-vol. reference work
45 Jacob's first wife
46 Not the original color
47 Soon-to-be grads: Abbr.
48 Company with an industrial average
50 Relentless nine-to-five gig, e.g.
53 "Norma ___"
54 "My gal" of song

55 Easiest to beat up
59 Yemeni seaport
61 Wrangler product
63 Toy dog, briefly
64 Coup d'___
65 "___ to the Moon" (first science fiction film, 1902)
66 Formerly, in old usage
67 Singer McEntire
68 Sheds feathers, e.g.

DOWN

1 Helps
2 ___ alone (have no help)
3 Concerning, in a memo
4 Explosive compound, in brief
5 More festive
6 Spanish rivers

7 Request
8 Appeared to be
9 Cuban coins
10 Ewe's cry
11 Confused situations
12 Bill Clinton was the first one elected president
13 Eye woes
18 Ordinary fellow
22 Thin
25 Record spinners . . . or a hint to 17-, 25-, 38-, 48- and 61-Across
26 Quick boxing punch
27 Cry of anticipation
28 One who mooches
29 How long the N.C.A.A. basketball tournament lasts
31 Architect Maya

34 Some potatoes
35 It protects the tympanic cavity
36 Rascals
39 Colorado tribe
42 Journey to Mecca
46 Undo, on a computer
48 Hang loosely
49 Perennial presidential candidate Ralph
51 Fix, as a printer's feeder
52 Connect with
55 Falafel bread
56 ___ of Sandwich
57 Vexed state
58 Baking soda amts.
60 Mesh
62 Arrest

by Oliver Hill

8

ACROSS

1 No-no
6 Late football star and FTD pitchman Merlin
11 Driver's lic. and such
14 Take forcibly
15 Sluggo's comics pal
16 Thing to pick
17 BAD
19 Buck's mate
20 Two cents' worth
21 Morales of "La Bamba"
22 Capitol Hill worker
23 BED
27 Name to the cabinet, say
30 Comic-strip light bulb
31 Van Susteren of Fox News
32 Ajax or Bon Ami
36 Weed whacker
37 BID
39 Movie pal of Stitch
40 Strange
42 River pair
43 At the drop of __
44 "Animal House" beanie sporters
46 BOD
50 Exclude
51 Late singer Horne
52 F.D.R. power project: Abbr.
55 Blood-type abbr.
56 BUD
60 Versatile vehicle, for short
61 For all to see
62 Not quite round
63 Place that's "up the river"
64 Hobbyist's knife brand
65 Doesn't hoof it

DOWN

1 Rolaids alternative
2 Province of ancient Rome
3 Like the proverbial beaver
4 Tolkien beast
5 Shakespeare character who goes insane
6 Having no intermission
7 "__ en Rose" (Edith Piaf song)
8 __-cone
9 Old French coin
10 Albany is its cap.
11 The movie "Wordplay," for one
12 L.E.D. part
13 High, pricewise
18 "This __ outrage!"

22 "Shane" star
23 Slow-cooked beef entree
24 Some flooring
25 Wroclaw's river
26 Neptune's realm
27 Ottoman Empire chief
28 "No __!" ("Easy!")
29 Hammer part
32 North-of-the-border grid org.
33 Rat on the Mob
34 Sommer in cinema
35 Woman depicted in "The Birth of Old Glory"
37 Neighbor of Yemen
38 Some are saturated
41 Letter after pi
42 Beat to death, so to speak

44 __ Vallarta, Mexico
45 Checkout annoyance
46 Like some toasters and children's books
47 Overdo it onstage
48 "Christ is __!" (Easter shout)
49 Say without thinking
52 Fly-catching creature
53 Show of hands, e.g.
54 Spy Aldrich
56 Symbol of slyness
57 Sch. founded by Thomas Jefferson
58 Gumshoe
59 56, in old Rome

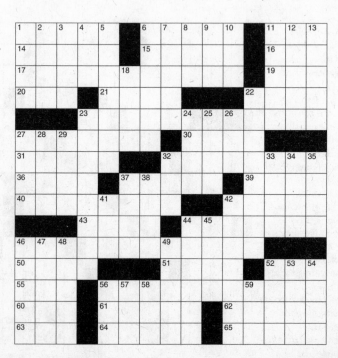

by Sarah Keller

ACROSS

1 "Hold it right there!"
5 Saintly glow
9 Scout's mission
14 Metrical foot
15 Pitcher
16 Prefix with centric
17 Mmes., in Madrid
18 Letterman of late-night
19 Anthracite and bituminous
20 See 40-Across
23 Bread for a ham sandwich
24 Saxophone and oboe
25 Elmer who hunts wabbits
27 Truth stretcher
30 Indian child
33 Suffix with serpent
34 Philanthropist
37 General Foods coffee
38 Party with leis
40 Subject of this puzzle
42 Hitch
43 Burst
45 Excite
47 Had lunch
48 Celebrate
50 Showing more age, maybe
52 Aware of
53 ". . . to fetch ___ of water"
55 Sal of song, e.g.
57 See 40-Across
62 Lasso
64 Wyatt of the West
65 Farm sounds
66 Bonehead
67 Predecessor of Exxon
68 Painting not for the demure
69 Phony gems
70 Like one side of a pool
71 "___ out?" (pet's choice)

DOWN

1 Bit of smoke
2 Spy Mata ___
3 Arabian Peninsula land
4 Soak up
5 Many an estate border
6 Oscar or Tony
7 501's
8 Calif. neighbor
9 Gets back
10 D.D.E.'s W.W. II command
11 See 40-Across
12 Left Turn ___ (street sign)
13 The scenter of things?
21 Ticked (off)
22 "___ Man Answers" (1962 flick)
26 "___ I say, not . . ."
27 Secretary, at times
28 Get used (to)
29 See 40-Across
30 Mice, to cats
31 In-line item
32 Itching to go
35 "Just do it" sloganeer
36 Start of a long distance call
39 Atop
41 Sweet drink
44 Test the strength of, chemically
46 Fussy sort
49 Miler Sebastian
51 Graduates
53 Humiliate
54 Derby prize
55 Handshake
56 Broadway hit co-written by Elton John
58 Owner's certificate
59 It could be proper
60 Extinct bird
61 River of Belgium
63 Preschooler

by Janice M. Putney

10

ACROSS
1 Fires
5 Pinup's legs
9 Hard to resolve
14 Away from the wind
15 Burn treatment
16 W.W. II conference site
17 "Not to worry!"
19 Super bargain
20 Big muddle
21 Join forces
23 Rap's Dr. ___
24 Early communications satellite
26 U.S. currency: Abbr.
27 "It's a snap!"
33 Part of the backbone
37 Cereal grain in Cap'n Crunch
38 Unwell, perhaps
39 Milk-Bone, e.g.
40 Request for a Milk-Bone?
41 Eyed impertinently
42 "___ well that ends well"
43 ___ nuevo
44 Unsettling
45 "Smooth sailing!"
48 Needlefish
49 Molded, as metal
54 Jefferson Davis was its pres.
57 Good to have around
59 Quebec's ___ Peninsula
60 First letter
62 "Like water off a duck's back!"
64 Port on the Korea Strait
65 Señor's affirmative
66 Duration
67 Last letter
68 Pitfall
69 "The Dukes of Hazzard" spinoff

DOWN
1 Art able to
2 Singly
3 Climbers' vacation spot
4 Lowly workers
5 Gossip
6 Glamour
7 Big name in faucets
8 Hard of hearing
9 Whitman's "Song of ___"
10 Dig in
11 Toy attached to a rope
12 Marquee-name entertainer
13 Part of the Ivy League
18 Production
22 Train whistle sound
25 Purpose
28 "Le Repos" artist
29 Zoo fixture
30 Qualified
31 Refuse to release
32 Small whirlwind
33 Baseball's Musial
34 Woody's musical son
35 Irishman or Welshman
36 Impulsive
40 Least likely to forgive
41 1980's Nicaraguan leader
43 Med. sch. course
44 DX divided by V
46 Spiny-crested lizard
47 "The ___ File" (Forsyth novel)
50 Kind of system
51 Colorado music festival site
52 Vice President Agnew
53 Abounds (with)
54 Mafia leader
55 Run-down area
56 Far end of a church
58 Den
61 Cauldron stirrer
63 Pup's bark

by Richard Hughes

ACROSS

1 When repeated, a shout when playing cowboy
5 Surmise
10 Picture problem
14 Chill
15 ___ Bornes (game)
16 Oral history
17 First spin: mixed fruit
20 Actress Monk of "N.Y.P.D. Blue"
21 Imposed on others' generosity
22 Complain
26 Pliable leather
27 Second spin: close, but no cigar
34 ___-Magnon
35 Drive on
36 Raconteur's offering
37 Slow down, in music: Abbr.
38 Visual way to communicate: Abbr.
39 Wallet cards, for short
42 Horatian composition
43 Hawaiian musicmakers
45 Surprising result
47 Relieve
48 Third spin: getting colder
52 Charged particle
53 Margaret Mead research site
54 Taxonomic category
58 Madrid museum
62 Fourth spin: jackpot!
66 Alexander II, e.g.
67 Santa ___, Calif.
68 Rasp
69 Walkman maker
70 Many times
71 Actor Montand

DOWN

1 Like some eagles
2 Tommie of the Miracle Mets
3 Deaden
4 Magazine founded by J.F.K. Jr.
5 Hobgoblin
6 Zero
7 Kind of shot
8 Tennyson's "immemorial ___"
9 Come back to, as a case
10 It may be carried for security's sake
11 Yearn
12 Impulse
13 College in Portland, Ore.
18 Land in C. S. Lewis's "Chronicles"
19 Somersault
23 Schools of thought
24 Flounce on a garment
25 "The Lady ___" (Henry Fonda film)
27 Cancel
28 Eleniak of "Baywatch"
29 Participant in democracy
30 Biblical prophet
31 New Zealander
32 Golden ___
33 Requirements
40 Consider
41 Barbershop sharpeners
44 Collection of seasonings
46 Software runners, briefly
49 Cut of meat
50 Paris-based org.
51 Refine further
54 British Airways fleet
55 100 centavos
56 Sen. Bayh
57 ___-help
59 Tel ___
60 Expunge
61 Vending machine inserts
63 Tank
64 Prior to
65 A Bobbsey twin

by David Bunker

ACROSS

1 Ex-leader of Iran
5 "Look over here!"
9 Part of an act
14 __ avail
15 Elevator inventor
16 Light bulb gas
17 On __ (needing no human intervention)
18 Diva Horne
19 If a = b and b = c, then a = c, e.g.
20 Scrabble space
23 Mess up
24 Chatter
25 Put fizz in
27 "__ Loves You"
29 Word after cream or powder
33 Jeanne or Thérèse: Abbr.
34 "__ la vista, baby!"
36 Necessity for an organ transplant
37 Clue space
40 Norelco product
41 Captured
42 Rd. or hwy.
43 Humdinger
44 Pop the question
45 Mother superior's charge
47 Aye's opposite
49 Computer department
50 Monopoly space
58 __ salts
59 Step on a ladder
60 Kind of hands that are "the devil's playthings"
61 Neutral shade
62 Sheltered
63 Rapid growth
64 Have a hunch
65 Kittens' cries
66 Split personalities?

DOWN

1 Free throw percentage, e.g.
2 2:00 or 3:00
3 Winter engine necessity
4 Ado
5 Vinelike vegetable
6 One-dish meal
7 __-American relations
8 Ex-leader of Russia
9 Lively dance music
10 Slow cooker
11 Breakfast food brand name
12 Film __
13 Suffix with refer
21 Superman enemy Lex __
22 Go blond, perhaps
25 Houston ballplayer
26 Patriot Allen
27 Porterhouse, e.g.
28 "Listen!"
30 Hardly ordinary
31 Strong point
32 Tender chicken
35 Fast fliers
36 Lions' den survivor
38 Food items served on sticks
39 Remnants
44 Author Rand
46 Writer for hire
48 Evangelist __ Semple McPherson
50 Soldiers in gray
51 Sporting blade
52 Z __ zebra
53 Tiny weight unit
54 Reign
55 Over
56 Soothing succulent
57 G.O.P.'s rivals

by Monica Krausse

ACROSS

1 H&R Block employees
5 Start
10 Yard sale caution
14 Present
15 With 26-Across, a Sri Lankan export
16 Actress Rowlands
17 Determines
19 When Hamlet dies in "Hamlet"
20 F.B.I. file
21 Walk softly
23 Familiar saying
26 See 15-Across
27 Not early or late
30 California wine valley
32 Pep rally shout
35 Spam, ham or lamb
36 "Under Siege" star Steven
38 George Gershwin's brother
39 When D.S.T. begins
40 Face-lift, e.g.
41 Balloon filler
42 It might go over your head
43 Last car?
44 Annoying insect
45 Pub pint
46 "¿Cómo ___ usted?"
47 "Steppenwolf" author
48 Elton John, since 1998
50 Frittata
53 Carpentry tool
56 Percussion instrument
60 Get better
61 Late, great violinist
64 Author Rice
65 Flick
66 Leave off
67 "Hey!"
68 Milky gems
69 "Name That Tune" clue

DOWN

1 Punch card fallout
2 Cuban currency
3 Parabolic paths
4 Escorts to the door
5 Chose
6 Approaches
7 Go downhill, maybe
8 Time in a waiting room, seemingly
9 Step in getting a license
10 Visibly shocked
11 Members of religious factions
12 Enthusiastic about
13 Goalie's goal
18 Irritate
22 It surrounds San Marino
24 17-Across or 11- or 29-Down, to 61-Across
25 Carries on
27 D-Day beach
28 Country with a five-sided flag
29 Followers of philosopher René
31 Scale down
33 Divas' offerings
34 Writer Bret
36 Litigates
37 Sister of Urania
40 Sex researcher Hite
44 Begin, slangily
47 Vanity plate in a two-car household
49 ___ of Langerhans
51 It might arrive with a beep
52 Parts of boxing gloves
53 Bloke
54 Nest egg protectors?
55 Bride and groom's vehicle
57 Office communiqué
58 Liverpudlian, e.g.
59 Pay for a hand
62 Drench
63 Gardner of film

by Peter Gordon

ACROSS

1 Go out
6 Understands
10 Put away
14 Big can producer
15 Door sign
16 Topological shapes
17 Finishing school enrollees
18 Danish toy company
19 Election losers
20 Carried too much?
23 Shoe part
25 Red Sox legend Williams
26 Kind of trip
27 Leopard, e.g.
28 Heroic tales
31 Construction element
33 Heroic tale
35 Strenuous class
36 Ike's W.W. II command
37 Quick, strong alcoholic drinks?
42 It may be positive or negative
43 Sass
44 "Pygmalion" playwright
46 ___ acid
49 Baseballer noted for bon mots
51 Bank offering, for short
52 Freight weight
53 Île ___ Marie
55 Modern Persians
57 Slap shots for Jagr or Lemieux?
61 Unwritten
62 Part of a horse's pedigree
63 Smell
66 Appropriately named Colorado county
67 Smell
68 Wild throw, e.g.
69 1950's P.M.
70 Top-of-the-hour radio offering
71 Spiteful

DOWN

1 Hang back
2 Ivy Leaguer
3 Clever verse
4 Latin for "I roll"
5 Stands in a studio
6 Shower soaps
7 Office honcho
8 Ballet wear
9 Non-P.C. garb
10 Desist
11 Something put on the spot?
12 Former Sandinista leader
13 Sagacity
21 President who was also a sportscaster
22 Bunker matriarch
23 Clinch
24 Refreshers, you might say
29 Swindle
30 Sufficient
32 Derisive reception
34 Gab
36 Zing
38 Tightenable loop
39 Yes or no follower
40 Academic types
41 Bombay wear
45 Used to be
46 Not out
47 Tied up, in a way
48 As a precaution
49 Next to
50 Come to light
54 Whom Holyfield KO'd, 11/9/96
56 Capital on the Gulf of Guinea
58 Hate group
59 Rooster's cry
60 His's partner
64 "___ so fast!"
65 Taste

by Richard Chisholm

ACROSS

1 Neighborhood
5 Press down, as pipe tobacco
9 Break one's silence
14 Not mom's
15 Villainous act
16 Spine-tingling
17 Top-quality
19 Scottish landowner
20 Roughly equal to one another
21 Like men at stag parties
23 Stage and screen actor ___ Ritchard
24 From years past
25 Former Yankee manager Joe
27 To wit
32 Pie ___ mode
35 Get ready to shoot again
37 Peter, Paul and Mary, e.g.
38 Point around which weight is evenly distributed
41 ___-Rooter
42 Necessitate
43 New: Prefix
44 Perplexer
46 Sword handles
48 Madison Avenue types
50 Mideastern princes: Var.
54 Ajax or Bon Ami
58 Electric train maker
59 Addiction
60 like all the letters in this clue
62 Bikini Island, e.g.
63 Sheep calls
64 Joint with a cap
65 Not at all relaxed
66 Totals up
67 Ooze

DOWN

1 Kind of committee
2 Seattle forecast
3 J. ___ Hoover
4 Fireplace receptacle
5 Guam, e.g.: Abbr.
6 Gardner of "On the Beach"
7 Politically moderate
8 Beseech
9 One-named Tejano singer
10 Sound, as bells
11 Keystone State port
12 Broadcasts
13 Popular sneakers
18 In abundance
22 Ivy feature
24 Wrinkle-resistant fabric
26 Peruses anew
28 Network with videos
29 Yeats's isle
30 Low-cal
31 Toy on a finger
32 Farm unit
33 Trotsky or Uris
34 The "A" of ABM
36 "Not you ___!?"
39 Dress (up)
40 Bright star, one corner of "the summer triangle"
45 Slugger Mickey
47 Lab garments
49 Peach follower, toast preceder
51 Asinine
52 Visit anew
53 Siesta
54 Web conversation
55 Recently deceased
56 Black, in poetry
57 Feels bad
58 Minus
61 Bit of chewing gum

by Holden Baker

16

ACROSS

1 Mayhem
6 French novelist André
10 White House dweller, informally
14 Madison Square Garden, for one
15 Yemeni port
16 New York's state flower
17 Desert bordering the Sinai
18 Shipshape
19 "I'm ___ here!"
20 Fed. property overseer
21 Organization for senior travelers
24 David of "Rhoda"
25 They make your time more valuable
26 Boston hub
31 Contents of Pandora's box
32 Years and years
33 Highchair attire
36 Pickling herb
37 ___ Nast
39 Second introduction?
40 Tack on
41 All there
42 Word that follows the start of 21-, 26-, 43- and 50-Across
43 Yellowish-brown
46 Host Conan
49 Literary ___
50 Edits
53 Expected
56 Half of zwei
57 Thug
58 Brief apology
60 Peevish humor
61 Writer Dinesen
62 Missouri River tributary
63 "The Awakening" protagonist
64 Snakelike fish
65 Olympics unit

DOWN

1 Put up on the wall
2 War deity
3 Lyra's brightest star
4 "A Chorus Line" number
5 Stalactite sites
6 Proponent of nonviolent protest
7 ___ fixe
8 Costly
9 Put in power
10 "To your health!"
11 Defeats decisively
12 Cosmetician Lauder
13 Enthusiasms
22 Mauna ___
23 Coxswain's command
24 Chutzpah
26 Zeus visited her as a swan
27 Exiled Latin poet
28 Embellish richly
29 Keep the issues coming
30 Pea's place
33 Roseanne, once
34 Concerning
35 Hopalong Cassidy portrayer Bill
37 Name on many libraries
38 "Not ___ bet!"
39 Glass tube filler
41 Put one's foot down
42 Bloom
43 Nap
44 Toasting sounds
45 Well-supplied resource?
46 Corpulent
47 Unquestioning, as faith
48 Altercation
51 Snoop (around)
52 Locomotive fuel
53 "Dadgummit!"
54 Craving
55 Observer
59 Sugar suffix

by Sarah Keller

ACROSS

1 IV units
4 Legal rights org.
8 1999 U.S. Open champ
14 Base stealer Brock
15 Not relevant
16 "Very well"
17 Roadie's burden
18 The "I" in "The King and I"
19 Major publicity
20 Workday evening, or a small medieval warrior
23 It's boring
24 Boxer's stat
25 Seventh heaven
27 "Dear" one
29 Not level
31 Vintage auto
32 Vehicle with a rotating top
34 Country singer Crowell
38 Harsh cry
39 Ultimate consumer
41 Horse-and-buggy ___
42 Ismail's title
44 Catbird seat?
45 "Impressive!"
46 Copper River's locale
48 Part of Nasdaq: Abbr.
49 Scratches
52 Rapscallion
55 1996 Madonna role
56 Flat-headed fastener, or Tiger's helpers
60 Indigenous
62 Hissy fit
63 "I like ___"
64 Like an aristocrat
65 Place to hole up
66 Originally named
67 Hardest to outwit
68 Hodgepodge
69 About 5 ml.

DOWN

1 Hammer feature
2 Draw near
3 January event, or a great bird
4 Appliance maker
5 Like dunce caps
6 Writing style
7 Where Logan is
8 Tough wood
9 Unselfish participant, or a mercantile harbor
10 Scrubbed
11 Brown shade
12 Met star Beverly
13 Peninsular land
21 Critical
22 Rolodex abbr.
26 Meltdown sites
27 Pinball paths
28 Lady's man
30 Shut out
32 Something to read, or blue-green overhangs
33 Year's record
35 Forest product, or the result of a second wind
36 Son of Aphrodite
37 [Ho-hum]
40 Like fresh strawberries
43 Felt
47 Sacramento-to–San Jose dir.
48 B & W film shower
49 Word on coins
50 Be of use
51 Frank known as "The Enforcer"
53 5th-century date
54 Nolan Ryan, notably
57 Capital near the 60th parallel
58 Scratches (out)
59 Break down
61 Summer D.C. setting

by Greg Staples

18

ACROSS

1 Replies to an invitation, briefly
6 Procrastinator's word
11 J.F.K.'s successor
14 Where to hear an aria
15 Stood up
16 Pitcher's stat.
17 Kids' bicycle features
19 Unhinged
20 List-ending abbr.
21 School grps.
22 Battery terminal
24 Bad golf drives
26 Eagle's claw
28 Bridge seat
30 Signed and delivered go-between
33 Church officer
36 Overwhelming defeat
38 Tortoise racer
39 Thumbs-up vote
40 Slob's opposite
43 Get a blue ribbon
44 Breaks bread
46 Thunderstruck
47 Lightens up
49 Extreme fears
51 Tennis great Ivan
53 Kind of force
55 Team listing
58 [Man, this is heavy!]
60 Panhandles
62 Spread for 8-Down
64 __ Grande
65 Big bang makers
68 Printer's need
69 Major artery
70 Laker Shaq
71 Hospital V.I.P.'s

72 Picked up on
73 Bogart classic "Key __"

DOWN

1 Morning garment
2 Tiffs
3 Easily bribed
4 Pecan treat
5 __ Antonio
6 What breaks a camel's back
7 Territory
8 Breakfast bread
9 Superlative suffix
10 Secondhand shop deal
11 Used car buyers' protection
12 Actor Pitt
13 Shade of green

18 Mimic
23 Wordsmith Webster
25 It's grown in ears
27 Italian wine region
29 Bellhop's locale
31 Canal of song
32 Scout groups
33 Looked at
34 Shakespearean king
35 Appointment organizers
37 College soph, e.g.
41 Opponent of 28-Across
42 Some sneakers
45 Poet Teasdale
48 Pennsylvania city

50 Classic yo-yo maker
52 Snoopy
54 Movie critic Roger
56 Bugs bugger Fudd
57 Sack again, as groceries
58 Dismal
59 Orange peel
61 Art Deco designer
63 Norwegian capital
66 "Yoo-___!"
67 Braz. neighbor

by Denise Neuendorf

ACROSS

1 Prefix with god
5 Start of a diary entry
9 Bona ___
14 Author Turgenev
15 French clergyman
16 Bonehead
17 Witty Bennett
18 No longer valid
19 Take in again
20 Immortality, of a sort
23 Laid, as a floor
24 Aborigine of Japan
25 Station launched in 1986
28 Treaty's aim
31 Docs united: Abbr.
34 People shoot it for fun
35 Parched
36 Lord's estate
38 Very
41 Flamboyance
42 Rows
43 Reply to a captain
44 What the devout have
49 Linkup of several PC's
50 Nine, in Nantes
51 Slipknot loop
54 Stamina
57 Ill will
60 Like a poor tennis player, frequently
61 Lawn mower maker
62 One of the Carpenters
63 Close
64 Idle of the Python troupe
65 Skillful
66 Pseudosophisticated
67 Intolerable smell

DOWN

1 They're spotted in casinos
2 100-meter hurdles, for one
3 ___ Gras
4 Completely
5 College near Charlotte
6 Coal-black
7 Mother of John Quincy
8 Freshwater minnow
9 Solidify, as plans
10 ___ fixe
11 Belittle, slangily
12 Help wanted abbr.
13 ___-Foy, Que.
21 Harvests
22 Filmmaker Lee
25 Actress Gibbs
26 How to respond to an affront
27 Color anew
29 Water temperature tester
30 Somme water
31 "Let's Make ___"
32 Kind of toast
33 With full force
37 Come to a halt
38 Tiny battery
39 Squeeze out, as a mop
40 Lens setting
42 Cop
45 It can be malicious
46 Teachers' org.
47 Venezuela neighbor
48 Owl
52 Talked impolitely
53 Weird
54 Dance instructor's call
55 Well-groomed
56 Sling missile
57 Jamaican music
58 Rocket launch site
59 Wrath

by Leonard Williams

20

ACROSS

1 1976 Best Picture
6 Discontinue
10 Tuna ___
14 Foolish
15 Thumbs-up write-up
16 Copycat
17 Affect strangely
18 "A Death in the Family" writer
19 Go all over
20 See 38-Across
23 Friend of Fidel
25 Voluminous ref. set
26 Minces
27 Churchill called it "soul-destroying"
30 Adversary
31 "Our Father which ___ heaven . . ."
32 Court entertainer
34 Plan of action
38 With 53-Across, a daffynition of 20-Across
41 Cicero's existence
42 Unsubstantial
43 Australian predator
44 Mess up
45 Military awards
46 Iroquois Confederacy tribe
50 Handle some hills
52 Get the picture
53 See 38-Across
57 Sported
58 Egg on
59 Flip response?
62 "What ___?"
63 Plotting
64 Angler's accessory
65 Fizzles out
66 They're crossable
67 Rash

DOWN

1 Part of a cage
2 Formula ___
3 Blockbuster rentals
4 Nautical unit
5 Mysterious Himalayan
6 Des Moines university
7 Fulminated
8 Done with
9 Resident's security device
10 His 1961 record had an asterisk
11 Historical period
12 River embankment
13 Lock of hair
21 New England catch
22 Charlotte of "The Facts of Life"
23 Overstarched collar problem
24 Long-eared animals
28 Good news on Wall Street
29 Business letter abbr.
30 Mossback
32 Place for a ride
33 Eight-time Norris Trophy winner
34 Footnote abbr.
35 Chou and others
36 Scout rank
37 Win by ___
39 Scolding
40 1952 political inits.
44 Old French coin
45 Russian for peace
46 Did some carpentry
47 Meat problem
48 Sip
49 Fencing needs
50 Union member
51 Praise
54 Text
55 Result of a bite, maybe
56 Mystery writer Paretsky
60 Court ruling?
61 Surreptitious

by Sarah Keller

ACROSS

1 Tennis's Arthur
5 Burn
10 "Ka-boom!"
14 Red light
15 Mark Twain forte
16 Arizona Indian
17 Middling
18 15-Across with a twist
19 Court cry
20 "Les Trois Mousquetaires" author
23 Actress Streep
24 Dem.'s foe
25 Information
29 Corporal, e.g.
34 Start of a quote from 20-Across
39 Prefix with surgery
40 Den
41 Rome's ___ Fountain
43 Brother of Cain
44 Montezuma, for one
46 More of the quote
48 Burn
50 Old autocrat
51 "Sweet as apple cider" girl
53 Op-ed piece
58 End of the quote
64 Lakers' O'Neal, informally
65 The March King
66 Nourishment
67 Lima's land
68 Start
69 Girl of Green Gables
70 "Star Wars" sage
71 Exigencies
72 Movie unit

DOWN

1 Area of India
2 Filched
3 One washing down a sidewalk, e.g.
4 Glue
5 Leg part
6 Congeal
7 God of love
8 Introvert
9 "Marriage A-la-Mode" playwright, 1672
10 To ___ it may concern
11 Georgetown athlete
12 Simians
13 Broadway's "Les ___"
21 Actor Ray
22 Over
26 Sotheby's stock
27 Bull in an arena
28 Concerning
30 Close
31 Where many Miamians were born
32 Baseball's Hershiser
33 Gangster's gal
34 It's said with a sigh
35 Lounge
36 Low-calorie
37 Worry
38 Day followers, in want ads
42 Dee/Darin film "___ Man Answers"
45 Voucher
47 Utah city
49 Inventor of the stock ticker
52 United
54 Up till now
55 Chief Justice, 1941–46
56 Expiate
57 Alpine call
58 Huxtable boy
59 Brain-busting
60 Greenish blue
61 River past Buckingham
62 Took advantage of
63 "Darn!"
64 Snoop (on)

by Richard Hughes

ACROSS

1 Evildoing Norse god
5 Get through one's head
10 Totally nuts
14 "___ go bragh"
15 Roast host
16 Greek war god
17 Make, as one's way
18 Horripilation
20 Motherless calf
22 Fix up
23 When Dijon is hot
24 Principal principles
28 Summer sign
30 Stick up
31 Many a Boy Scout
32 Sun or moon
33 Garfield's foil
35 "We're in trouble"
39 Shirley Jones sitcom, with "The"
44 Son of Isaac
45 Latch (onto)
46 "Waking ___ Devine" (1998 film)
47 Thai cash
51 "Chances ___"
52 Anonymous John
53 Las Palmas locale
58 Foreman KO'er
59 Fast time
60 Bores, informally
63 Sorter's slot
67 Taj Mahal locale
68 Sonar comeback
69 Composer Copland
70 Timely question?
71 Gels
72 Stand in good ___
73 Eye affliction

DOWN

1 Not decent
2 Stackable cookie
3 Largest venomous snake
4 Kipling setting, often
5 Trip segment
6 Comic Philips
7 Something squirreled away
8 Move to the front row, maybe
9 Tone arm attachment
10 Guy's date
11 Staggering
12 "Beau ___"
13 Hibachi residue
19 Driver's warning
21 Bad throw, e.g.
25 ___ al-Fayed (friend of Diana)
26 Footnote abbr.
27 Latin word on a penny
28 Run easily
29 Stretches of time
34 Bird-to-be
36 It may be 20-20
37 Toast topper
38 London's ___ Park
40 Big brass
41 Lander at Ben-Gurion
42 "My kingdom ___ horse!"
43 Make better
48 A Guthrie
49 "Laughing" scavengers
50 G.I.'s headgear, slangily
53 Bullfighters' accessories
54 Ralph's missus
55 Time for some shifts
56 Keep for later
57 Many chess outcomes
61 The hunted
62 Of sound mind
64 Dawn goddess
65 Mauna ___
66 Finis

by Barbara Olson

ACROSS

1 Home of Goodyear
6 Go well together
10 Unappetizing cafeteria serving
14 Severe Athenian lawmaker
15 "For a long and healthy life" sloganeer
16 Spot for a comb
17 Halloween success story?
19 Gen. Bradley
20 It comes out of a pen
21 Pine dripping
22 Hymn
23 Corn feature
25 8:00–8:30, e.g., on a schedule
27 Skin-covered canoe
30 Foolish
34 RCA or EMI
37 Scene setters
39 European car
40 Free-for-all
41 "What's ___ for me?"
42 It's still made
44 Affirm
45 Gong
46 Like Halloween candy in December
48 Dental school exam?
50 AAA, maybe
54 Pickling liquid
57 They come out of pens
60 Lawyers' org.
61 Radio format
62 Halloween shrub?
64 Lotion ingredient
65 Field

66 Like a maple leaf
67 Plead innocent to
68 Cologne mister
69 Utterances of "Trick or treat"?

DOWN

1 "You have to ___ . . ."
2 Swedish money
3 Puts first or second, say
4 Place for future Lts.
5 Fake
6 Sci-fi setting
7 Like some textbook publishers
8 Whirls
9 Baking
10 Halloween correspondent?
11 City founded by Pizarro
12 Racetrack
13 Wave maker
18 Sinuous
22 Fishing site
24 Item on a Halloween ring?
26 Perry of "90210"
28 Help at a holdup
29 Cabbage types
31 St. Columba's island
32 Polish's partner
33 Direction in which el sol rises
34 Upper story
35 Samoan capital
36 Wall of earth
38 U.S.D.A. stamp abbr.

40 Person who hears "goo-goo"
43 Item of merchandise
44 Greatly reduced
47 Egyptian cross
49 French river
51 Blade holder
52 Overweight
53 Dylan Thomas's home
54 Thin nail
55 Lady Macbeth, e.g.
56 Click site
58 Roman way
59 Tar Heel State: Abbr.
62 Comic strip cry
63 Coach Parseghian

by Mary Pat Hidding

ACROSS

1 Muscle that a runner stretches
5 Bullets
9 Dictation taker
14 Land east of the Urals
15 Friend to Androcles
16 Pavarotti or Carreras
17 58-Across player in 1917
19 Rust, e.g.
20 Ready
21 French head
22 Clearings
23 58-Across player in 1953
26 Serve to be reserved
27 "Oh, brother!"
28 Pinup's leg
31 Wife
34 No-no for Mrs. Sprat
36 Woke up, with "to"
37 58-Across player in 1963
40 Phi __ Kappa
41 Sub __ (in secret)
42 2001's symbol, in the Chinese calendar
43 Boozer
44 Opposite of bellum
45 Municipal council member: Abbr.
46 58-Across player in 1946
51 Printed cloth
54 World's longest river
55 Canon camera
57 One way to be taken
58 Queen of the 54-Across
60 Punitive
61 Like many Mae West quotes
62 Gal's dream date
63 Rubberneck
64 What extra innings break
65 Church recess

DOWN

1 Be-boppers
2 Whence the phoenix rises
3 Deceive
4 Macarena or Beanie Babies, once
5 Even if
6 Sporty Mazda
7 Edible mushroom
8 __ roll (lucky)
9 Swiped
10 Either President Bush
11 Writer Bagnold
12 Junction point
13 Valuable deposits
18 Goddess of wisdom and war
22 Concede, as a point
24 Public square
25 Nebraska's first capital
28 Big bash
29 In a frenzy
30 No more than
31 Attic sights
32 Butter substitute
33 Catcher's catcher
34 Pope of 1605
35 Aliens, for short
36 Pop star Lauper
38 Cry at La Scala
39 In Morpheus' arms
44 Predicament
45 Metallic mixtures
46 Parish priest
47 China's Zhou __
48 Nephew's sister
49 Fancy duds
50 Taxi tooters
51 Tams
52 Help in crime
53 Sweater girl Turner
56 Rice wine
58 PC screen: Abbr.
59 "Now I get it!"

by Jenny Gutbezahl

ACROSS

1 Place to kick an addiction
6 Manager-of-the-Month, e.g.
11 Auction action
14 Big game venue
15 Like Peary's exploration
16 Prefix with therm
17 One who switches political affiliation?
19 "I didn't know that!"
20 Mao ___-tung
21 Oases' features
22 Big name at Indy
24 Genesis event, with "the"
25 At the summit of
26 Convention writer's footwear?
31 Cowboy bucker
32 Jackie O's man
33 Shoelace problem
35 54, in old Rome
36 Doesn't quite tell
40 Batman and Robin, e.g.
41 Feds
43 Poppycock
44 Board for nails
46 Red, white and blue, for Americans?
50 Read electronically
51 Up to it
52 Funt of "Candid Camera"
54 Tax cheat's risk
56 Little piggy
59 By way of
60 One who tries to sell a political slate?

63 007 creator Fleming
64 White heron
65 Slowly, in music
66 Rapper Dr. ___
67 Loamy deposit
68 Rocker John

DOWN

1 Engrossed
2 Historical times
3 "Take one!"
4 Colony crawler
5 TV series set on Malibu Beach
6 Harlem theater
7 Winter wear
8 Matterhorn and others
9 Sally Field's "Norma ___"
10 Longtime radio advice-giver
11 Profligate
12 Visionary's words
13 Go-getter
18 Ill-gotten gain
23 Breakfast area
24 Word before mail or tail
25 Where 37-Down is
26 Groom oneself
27 Parking place?
28 Wretched
29 Lady's title
30 Whiskey drinks
31 Common lunch order
34 Kind of poodle
37 Land on the Strait of Hormuz

38 ". . . ___ a lender be"
39 Betraying
42 Likable
45 Larry and Curly's chum
47 Place for a vase
48 Starfleet Academy students
49 Passing notice
52 Enthusiastic
53 Pinocchio, at times
54 Field measure
55 Luau instruments
56 Pitched item
57 Not fooled by
58 Berkshire school
61 "Where did ___ wrong?"
62 Salon stuff

by Denise Neuendorf

ACROSS

1 N.H.L. division: Abbr.
4 Is wearing
9 With 11-Down, "Casablanca" site
14 Word with caddy or bag
15 Prefix with arthritis
16 Online sales
17 ___ sgt. (police rank)
18 "Never!"
20 They undergo bonding
22 Glossy finish
23 Angry parent's yell
27 Patricia of "Breakfast at Tiffany's"
28 Order members
29 Political cartoonist Rall
32 Pindar, for one
34 Enlarged river, perhaps
37 Connie Francis's 1960 film debut
41 Have no more good ideas
42 Sticks
43 "Undoubtedly"
44 Resentments
45 Discharge
49 Comment about a sad but memorable exit
53 Numbskulls
55 Michael who starred in TV's "It's a Great Life"
56 1975 Four Seasons hit
60 Legal rep.
61 Exuded
62 "Today" co-host
63 Strive (for)
64 Newspaper opinion pieces
65 Drops out of the bidding
66 Summer in Sèvres

DOWN

1 When many duels take place
2 Raise canines?
3 One of the Jacksons
4 "Want to explain that?"
5 Silvery gray
6 Sault ___ Marie
7 Wine: Prefix
8 Hotel lobby sign
9 Splendid
10 Words to elicit recognition
11 See 9-Across
12 Waste, as time
13 Insidious
19 Some acct. money
21 Royal address?
24 Kwanzaa principle
25 Heavy drinker
26 Acura model
29 American acquisition of 2001
30 Musician's gift
31 Purchase for a disguise
33 "___ Rosenkavalier"
34 "El Capitán" composer
35 Looker
36 They may be fixed
37 Lopsided, as a grin
38 Color
39 Dash widths
40 Mishandled
44 A thing unto ___
46 Native Arizonan
47 "That makes sense!"
48 Exactly
49 Enticed
50 Engine covers
51 Off-road goer, briefly
52 Traditional letter closer
53 Breakfast place, for short
54 Drift (off)
56 Try to win over
57 ___ Tiago
58 Actor Brynner
59 Multivolume ref.

by Brendan Emmett Quigley

ACROSS

1 Mimic
5 20-20, e.g.
9 Bookcase part
14 As a rule
16 Place for a cookout
17 One . . .
19 City near Oberhausen
20 Bygone U.S. gas name
21 Prepares, as leather
22 Roam (about)
24 New York archbishop Edward
26 Chemical term after poly-
29 Pro ___ (proportionately)
31 Pocket watch attachment
34 Teen affliction
35 "Moonstruck" actress
37 ___ the Greek
39 Three . . .
42 1966 movie or song
43 1960's–70's singer Marvin
44 "___ a man with seven wives"
45 Gridiron official, for short
46 Work like ___
48 Magritte and Clair
50 Indonesian island
52 Dot follower
53 Each
55 Not good, but not bad
58 New moon, for one
63 Five . . .
66 Hull parts
67 Flower with a bulb
68 Liability's opposite
69 Toy that does tricks
70 Pear-shaped instrument

DOWN

1 Commedia dell'___
2 Where hymnals are stored
3 They can get in the way of a deal
4 Unsophisticated sort
5 Middle X of X-X-X
6 Bothered
7 Building wings
8 Gets rid of the gray
9 Snoop
10 "___ luego"
11 Wharton novel
12 Great Britain's emblem
13 Rivals
15 Suddenly run (at)
18 ___ et Chandon (Champagne)
23 Bow
25 Peer (at)
26 French place of education
27 Tobacco holders
28 Actress Garr
29 Label anew
30 Painterish
32 Double reeds
33 Simpson boy
34 Come from ___
36 Novelist Victor
38 Valhalla host
40 Flippered animal
41 Life saver
47 Tiddlywink, e.g.
49 Gas gauge warning
51 Macintosh maker
52 One's share of a medical bill, maybe
53 "___ silly question . . ."
54 Mincemeat desserts
56 Green-light
57 Japanese wrestling
59 Bunker ___
60 Rights org.
61 Playlet
62 In ___ (existing)
64 Follower: Suffix
65 Like a B'way hit

by Janice M. Putney

ACROSS

1 Great buy
6 Bar in a kitchen
10 Twinkle-toed
14 Major gold exporter of Africa
15 Fully fit
16 Campus hangout
17 Carpet fasteners
18 Dry run
19 "Battle Cry" novelist
20 Start of a riddle
23 Successes
24 Scale abbr.
25 "Thank U" singer Morissette
29 Middle of the riddle
33 Pierced places
34 Poker declaration
37 Kanga's kid
38 End of the riddle
42 The Pointer Sisters' "__ So Shy"
43 Vichyssoise ingredient
44 Came up
45 With 52-Across, answer to the riddle
48 Goings-on
49 Drama in Kyoto
50 Lot of loot
52 See 45-Across
58 Beat to a pulp
59 Long for
60 "The Cider House Rules" Oscar winner
62 Guesstimate words
63 Aware of
64 Around-the-world trip
65 Catty comment
66 Stink
67 Gardeners' woes

DOWN

1 Pepper, for one
2 Sign of spring
3 A throw
4 "Puppy Love" singer
5 Something that may be asked from bed
6 Squelched
7 Listens to
8 What's more
9 Prone to pique
10 Racket game
11 Knit one, __ two
12 Means of shipping
13 QB's gains: Abbr.
21 Bad-mouth
22 "Murder, She Wrote" airer
25 __ Phi Omega
26 Misplaces
27 Deep cavity
28 Computer giant
30 Fabric that travels well
31 Friars Club event
32 Weighty books
34 Swelling reducer
35 "The Simpsons" bartender
36 Publicity, say
39 Bad spirits
40 Go ballistic
41 Prior to, to Prior
46 "You said a mouthful!"
47 It's passed in a sénat
48 Pipe joint
50 Cheap jewelry
51 Reassuring words
52 Stud's mate
53 Exxon predecessor
54 Greedy cry
55 Hard to find
56 Bronx cheer
57 Camelot lady
58 Celebrated apple-pie maker
61 S.A.T. company

by Nancy Salomon and Bob Peoples

29

ACROSS
1 Under lock and key
5 Hits to the stands
10 Outstanding
14 "___ cost you"
15 Severe spasm
16 Part of "S.N.L."
17 Homecoming attendee
18 "The Cloister and the Hearth" author Charles
19 Created a caricature
20 "Bye Bye, Love" star, 1995
23 Snare
24 Brawl
27 Work the wheel
28 Becky Thatcher's creator
32 Dog-___
33 "Understood"
34 Hardly a brawl
35 Theme of this puzzle
38 Trunk growth
42 What have-nots have
43 Styx site
48 "Beverly Hills 90210" actor
50 Modern-day horse-and-buggy travelers
51 One of Chekhov's "Three Sisters"
52 P.D.Q.
53 Notorious 1930's bank robber
58 Urge (on)
60 Strange
61 Gold-coated
62 South American capital
63 South American animal

64 Market
65 Pounds' sounds
66 Like a sleeping bag or a swimming pool
67 Cafeteria item

DOWN
1 Like Anna's students
2 Peach Bowl venue
3 What eyes and moths do
4 Victim of a Dutch disease
5 Bug in one's throat?
6 Cry after a close call
7 William Saroyan's "My Name Is ___"

8 Hoo-ha
9 Plant-to-be
10 Hardly the latest buzz
11 Bug a phone
12 First mate?
13 Dawn droplets
21 Feature of Greece but not Germany
22 Suffix with panel
25 Argentine aunt
26 Neighbor of Que.
28 No gleeful giver
29 In accordance with
30 How saxes sound
31 Nickelodeon's "Kenan & ___"
36 "Blastoff!" preceder
37 Lewis with Lamb Chop

38 11th-century date
39 Word before Father or Lady
40 Winter Olympics sight
41 Married Madrileñas
44 Surrounded by
45 More run-down
46 Dickens girl
47 Soon
49 Tuba note?
52 Argue at the bar
54 Dickens girl
55 Site for slicers
56 Zagros Mountains locale
57 Pucker producer
58 Devious
59 Zadora of "Hairspray"

by Frank A. Longo

ACROSS

1 [Uh-oh!]
5 Lawn mower's path
10 Subway Series team
14 Andy Taylor's TV son
15 2008 Summer Olympics host
16 Burn soother
17 Shock
20 Temporary
21 Sly looks
22 Tombstone inscription
23 Physically weak
26 Canyon sound
29 Eagle's claw
31 Experiment sites
35 Garbage
37 Bronco-riding event
39 Quick swim
40 Behave oddly
43 Eden woman
44 Entered, as a car
45 Funny bone's location
46 Monthly budget item
48 Dukes
50 Cub Scout groups
51 Respond to a stimulus
53 Skirt's edge
55 Black key above a G
58 Popular Toyota
62 Definitely deceased
66 Pulitzer-winning humorist Barry
67 Video game name
68 Jane Austen novel
69 Constellation part
70 Neighbor of Oman
71 Thumbs-up votes

DOWN

1 Mongolian desert
2 Fairy tale's second word
3 Light, happy tune
4 Baseball player with the most lifetime hits
5 Screenwriter's writing
6 "For __ the Bell Tolls"
7 Eye the bull's-eye
8 Explosive initials
9 "So there!"
10 Old phone company nickname
11 Model Macpherson
12 __ de France
13 Views
18 Part of T.G.I.F.: Abbr.
19 Inventor Whitney
23 Busy person on Valentine's Day
24 Chinchilla or beaver, e.g.
25 From the top
26 Bygone anesthetic
27 Hunger for
28 Place of refuge
30 Colder than cold
32 Pueblo brick
33 Yellowstone animal
34 Gushes
36 Witch
38 Bullring cheer
41 Divan
42 Inherited wealth
47 Stock exchange worker
49 One who's way ahead in the polls
52 Greek vowel
54 Flub
55 Uses an abacus
56 Achievement
57 Output of Mount Etna
58 Apple leftover
59 Weak, as an excuse
60 Peru's capital
61 "What a pity!"
63 Articulate
64 Took in takeout?
65 Beaver's work

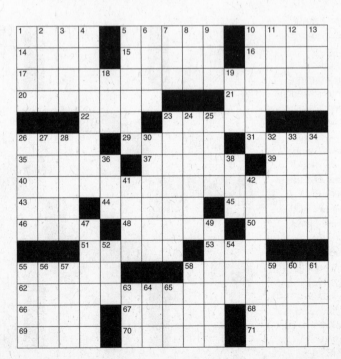

by Peter Gordon

ACROSS

1 Labor Day and many other fed. holidays
5 Canterbury can
9 "Auld Lang ___"
13 Eastern nurse
14 Slow, on a score
15 Where homeys hang
16 Lamb's meat made of building blocks?
18 Got on in years
19 Six Flags New England locale
20 Utah state flower
22 For most movie audiences
24 ___ y Plata (Montana's motto)
25 Decision regarding a Belafonte song?
31 Picture holder
34 1989 Oscar winner Jessica
35 Susan of "The Partridge Family"
36 Guilty one, in copspeak
37 Lion tamers' needs
38 Wine label info
39 Sister of Zsa Zsa
40 Sound on the hour
41 Totaled, costwise
42 Place for assenting Brits?
45 Ltd., here
46 Foxhole occupant
50 Guaranteed to work
55 Sen. Feinstein
56 Airline since 1948
57 Beatle's maxim?
59 Add fringe to
60 Subordinate Clauses?
61 Oozy ground
62 Hammer or sickle
63 Roy Rogers's real surname
64 Rose part

DOWN

1 Of the cheek
2 Alpha's opposite
3 Bother persistently
4 Made the scene
5 Comprehend
6 Black or red insects
7 Platte River Indian
8 A million to one, say
9 Haifa hello
10 One who sits cross-legged, maybe
11 Christmas
12 Water awhirl
14 Like inferior gravy
17 Sir's mate
21 Unrestrained revelry
23 Like some romances
26 "I love," to Yvette
27 Sets free
28 Genesis garden
29 "Cool!"
30 Newbie
31 Mimic
32 First name in jeans
33 Toot one's own horn
37 "So?"
38 Sail supports
40 Boxes: Abbr.
41 Kindled anew
43 Campus Jewish organization
44 Fusses
47 Mukluks wearer
48 ___ nous
49 Shorten again, perhaps
50 Pedal pushers
51 Designer Gucci
52 Othello's ensign
53 Plug up
54 A deadly sin
58 "How about that!"

by Kelly Clark

ACROSS

1 Clinched, with "up"
5 Teach at a college?
9 Zoological feet
14 Maui bash
15 Uninspired teaching method
16 ___ Perot
17 Idle in a "circus"
18 River to the Rhine
19 Cries of pain
20 Early White House hostess
23 Part of a figure eight
24 Noted film, as old Romans would have it
25 Co. that makes a bunch?
28 1986 Huey Lewis and the News hit
32 "Sold out" sign
34 Propel, in a way
35 Bargain hunter's haunt
36 Muscled one
39 It's run up and then settled
41 Conger hunter
42 Wildcat
44 Gangster's piece
46 Suffix with Peking
47 Urban luxury
51 Tucson-to-Flagstaff dir.
52 Part of E.T.A.: Abbr.
53 Time on end
54 Team hinted at by 20-, 28- and 47-Across
61 West Indian sorcery
63 Half a fortnight
64 Chemist's amount
65 Tehrani's tongue
66 Years abroad
67 Bog
68 It's to your advantage
69 Wine choice
70 Competent

DOWN

1 Enjoy some winter fun
2 Continental capital
3 Mourn out loud
4 Physics centers
5 Beseeches
6 Not stay put
7 Not this or that, below the border
8 What a dog's bark or cat's meow may mean
9 Mr. Universe's pride
10 Switch back?
11 Ruined
12 Immigrant's course: Abbr.
13 Draft org.
21 Like-thinking, for short
22 "___ in Love With You"
26 Arborist's concern
27 Raison ___
28 Nonrenters
29 ___ grass
30 Confederate general who won at Chickamauga
31 Western Indian
32 Hairless, now
33 Military mission, briefly
37 TV ET
38 Opposite of all
40 Ovine line?
43 Whig's rival
45 Person who might speak Klingon
48 Hawkish
49 Put on
50 Stumper
55 Facility
56 City at the foot of the Sierra Nevada
57 Grasps
58 Toddler's place
59 First name in Communism
60 "Peter Pan" role
61 Son ___ gun
62 Undergrad degs.

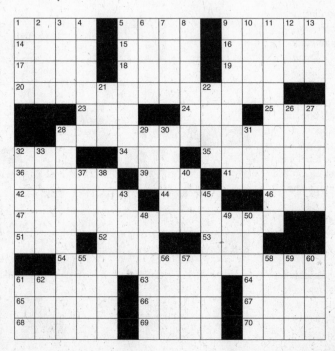

by M. Francis Vuolo

ACROSS

1 Oregon's capital
6 Sounds worked on by speech therapists
11 With 69-Across, a film with 27- and 64-Across
14 Appliance maker
15 Immobile
16 Wire service inits.
17 27- and 64-Across film, with "The"
19 Wager
20 W.W. II area: Abbr.
21 Principles
22 Risqué
23 A nonmusician may have one
25 Exude
27 Half of a famous Hollywood duo
33 Place for a breath of fresh air?
36 Wriggly fish
37 Precisely
38 Give __ time
40 Mo. with Columbus Day
42 Giant
43 Dummies
45 Rankle
47 Unhip person
48 27- and 64-Across film
51 Certain legal protection
52 Difficult experience
56 Outlaws
59 "__ Fideles"
62 Untruth
63 "Who __ we kidding?"
64 Other half of the Hollywood duo
66 Half a dozen
67 Go out with __
68 Bury
69 See 11-Across
70 Pianist Hess and others
71 Poor

DOWN

1 TV comic Bob
2 Celebrated Italian violinmaker
3 Apply, as a coat of wax
4 Epilogue
5 Rum cocktail
6 MGM symbol
7 Regarding
8 Pie chart part
9 Arrange by ZIP code, e.g.
10 Fr. holy woman
11 Oompah instrument
12 Assn. with many Gulf members
13 Feel sorry for
18 "From the Earth to the Moon" writer
22 Put on again, as weight
24 Appetizers with sweet-and-sour sauce
26 Kind of suit
28 1980's–90's car name
29 Spanish hero who died in 1099
30 Suffix with cigar
31 Behind
32 Transmit
33 Boys
34 "This looks bad"
35 Nothin'
39 Meat slicer site
41 __-la-la
44 Believe in wholeheartedly
46 Ship speed units
49 Make beloved
50 Obtuse one
53 A-list types
54 Broadcast
55 Apprehensive
56 Big party
57 Opera excerpt
58 Cashier's cry
60 Dame __, Barry Humphries character
61 Droops
64 Mom, dad and the kids: Abbr.
65 Gas suffix

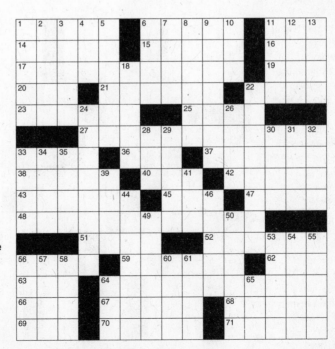

by Bette Sue Cohen

ACROSS

1 Go soft
5 Meter reading
9 Stogie
14 Home to billions
15 "Think nothing
___"
16 Eyes
17 Done in
desperation
19 Dismissed
20 Walk quietly
21 Moray, for one
23 Dele canceler
24 Olympic sled
26 Whippers
28 Unlike 1/2
32 Equal
33 Mal de ___
34 "Horrible" comics
character
36 Painter Max
39 Mars's Greek
counterpart
41 Highway
behemoths
43 Race's finish line
44 Gin's go-with
46 Odd-numbered
page
48 Preceded
49 Bygone autocrat
51 Sticks in the
snow?
53 Domains of
influence
56 Dance unit
57 "Your Show of
Shows" regular
58 ___ canto
(singing style)
60 Come up with
64 Arizona home
66 Surfer's stop?
68 Iranian money
69 Shredded
70 Gossip tidbit

71 Clotho, Lachesis
and Atropos
72 "Ars amatoria"
poet
73 Thomas Hardy
heroine

DOWN

1 Brewery supply
2 Actor Morales
3 Saying "th"
for "s"
4 Spill the beans
5 Pâté meat
6 Back at sea?
7 Houston university
8 Neighbor of Lucy
9 Rank above maj.
10 Polar cover
11 Not-so-super
bowl?

12 "Ragged Dick"
author
13 Major melees
18 Moolah
22 Drink like a dog
25 Rarin' to go
27 Use a needle
28 "___ my wit's end!"
29 Detective Wolfe
30 Attire popular
with private eyes
31 Fabrics with
metallic threads
35 "Casablanca" cafe
37 Sporting blade
38 Cinergy Field
athletes
40 Large
42 Like letters on
shirts
45 Geo or Reo

47 Kiri Te Kanawa's
milieu
50 Gray-clad soldier
52 Gift-giver's request
53 Winter accessory
54 Lecterns
55 Argument
59 Ukrainian city
near the Polish
border
61 Prefix with date
62 Golfers' needs
63 Shade trees
65 Coveted
Scrabble tile
67 Dernier ___

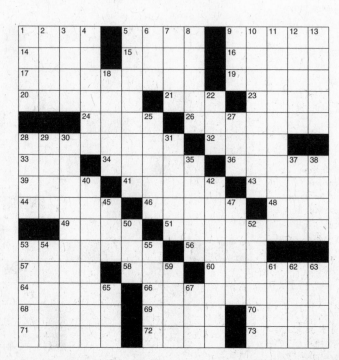

by Ed Early

ACROSS

1 Skein formers
6 It may be checkered
10 Having no depth
14 Shrimp's kin
15 Emmy winner Falco
16 Seer's garb
17 Splendor of Leeds's river?
19 March 17 slogan word
20 Fax user
21 Bygone comic strip
23 Part of Q.E.D.
25 "So's __ old man!"
26 Chest muscles, briefly
29 __ long way (last)
31 Holiday Inn rival
36 Turkish bigwig
37 Henry of "Fail-Safe"
39 "Olympia" painter Édouard
40 Reason for bad performance reviews?
43 __ Martin (car)
44 Inventor Howe
45 I.C.U. hookups
46 Places for fans
48 Easy threesome?
49 Coffeehouse performer
50 Capt.'s inferiors
52 "__ small world!"
54 Old Buicks
59 High spirits
63 In a dead heat
64 General issue facegear?
66 Receipt stamp
67 Stereotypical hunchback
68 Any "Seinfeld" episode, now
69 Word before a discounted price
70 Darkroom images, for short
71 Ore carriers

DOWN

1 Transcript figs.
2 Ashtabula's lake
3 Pull down
4 Ingmar and Ingrid Bergman
5 Bitter-__ (diehard)
6 Dispenser candy
7 Wood-dressing tool
8 Like a river bottom
9 Be about to fall
10 Tough journey
11 Sported
12 Passing mention?
13 Item for an insurance examiner
18 Catherine of __
22 A Musketeer
24 1,000 kilograms
26 Half a 60's vocal foursome
27 Cast out
28 Magna __
30 __ Rogers St. Johns
32 1960 World Series hero, familiarly
33 1/22/44 beachhead
34 Dig deeply
35 Alamogordo event
37 Touch lovingly
38 Out
41 Potential heir
42 Statement of what's known, in legalese
47 Muscle problem
49 W.W. II tank
51 One giving marching orders
53 Sudden burst
54 Auction vehicle, often
55 Turgenev or Boesky
56 Prop for Salome
57 Race place, familiarly
58 Urban problem
60 Pound of literature
61 Squalid digs
62 Burns and Allen: Abbr.
65 Soph. and jr.

by Fred Piscop

ACROSS

1 It's just one of those things
5 "Aw, shucks" expressions
10 More
14 Jealous wife in Greek myth
15 Slackened
16 A portion
17 "The moan of doves in immemorial ___": Tennyson
18 Campbell of "Martin"
19 Winter Palace ruler
20 Ready to swoon
23 "Go on . . ."
24 Clan emblem
25 Straight start?
27 Orbital periods
29 Actor McKellen
31 Birth control device
32 C.P.R. administrator
34 It ends in Mecca
35 Brit. legislators
36 Good-looking
40 Insulation ingredient, for short
41 Cooperstown nickname
42 Wool source
43 Bolo, for one
44 Michael Jordan's alma mater, in brief
45 Have it ___
49 Place for rings
51 Gives the gate
55 Genetic letters
56 Seedy-looking
59 ___ fide
60 Baptism and bris
61 L.A. gang member
62 Need a bath badly
63 Awaited a dubbing
64 Surrealist Magritte
65 Charger, to a Cockney
66 Lowly ones
67 Took habitually

DOWN

1 Tao, literally
2 Curtis of hair care
3 Loser of 1588
4 What to do?
5 "I ___ kick . . ."
6 Grammy winner Bonnie
7 Joe Jackson's "___ Really Going Out With Him?"
8 Book after Ezra
9 Minn. neighbor
10 Fruity-smelling compound
11 Experience a delay
12 They attract rubberneckers
13 Musket attachment
21 "C'mon, I wanna try!"
22 Gentile
26 Some E.R. cases
28 ___ judicata
30 "Song of the South" song syllables
33 Unable to decide
34 Shaker ___, O.
36 Satanic sort
37 Colorless solvents
38 Addictive stuff
39 Japanese capital
40 School grp.
46 Strasbourg siblings
47 Like lots of shopping now
48 Sang like Satchmo
50 Not out
52 Complete
53 Cliff projection
54 They may come in batteries
57 Torah holders
58 L'eggs shade
59 Term of address in the 'hood

by M. Francis Vuolo

ACROSS

1 "It's us against ___"
5 Backtalk
9 Data disk
14 What an optimist always has
15 This, south of the border
16 Bakery enticement
17 The "U" in I.C.U.
18 Larger ___ life
19 Circus star with a whip
20 1966 Johnny Rivers hit
23 Doozy
24 Suffix with pay or play
25 Capt.'s superior
28 Rock band ___ Mode
31 Cinder
34 Yale of Yale University
36 "Just ___ thought!"
37 Chorus member
38 Hospital ward alternative
42 Pentagon inventory
43 "Tip-Toe Thru the Tulips With Me" instrument
44 Make up (for)
45 Mudhole
46 Israeli parliament
49 Gave supper
50 ___-Cat (winter vehicle)
51 Currier's companion
53 1998 Best Picture nominee
60 Attacks
61 Opposed to, in dialect

62 Annapolis inits.
63 Tour of duty
64 Oodles
65 ___ for oneself
66 Short-tempered
67 As a result
68 Lawyers' charges

DOWN

1 As a result
2 Sharpen, as on a whetstone
3 "Ben-Hur," e.g.
4 Geo model
5 Medium-sized sofa
6 Equivalent to B flat
7 Dateless
8 Levelheaded
9 Longhorns, e.g.
10 Pulitzer Prize category
11 Capital of Italia
12 Gathering clouds, for one
13 Ruin
21 Turn out to be
22 Like a rare baseball game
25 Monument Valley features
26 On the ball
27 Force open, as a lock
29 Place for icicles
30 Civil War side: Abbr.
31 Standoffish
32 Slingshot ammo
33 ___ in on (neared)
35 Towel stitching
37 College major
39 Kind of sentence

40 Mamie's man
41 Moth-___
46 Hard to saw, as some pine
47 What a stucco house doesn't need
48 Be that as it may
50 Meager
52 Cram
53 After curfew
54 Sale caution
55 Doom
56 Composer Stravinsky
57 "Now it's clear"
58 Shakespeare's ___ Hathaway
59 Boys
60 Monogram of 40-Down's predecessor

by Gregory E. Paul

ACROSS

1 Farmland unit
5 News source of old
10 Summer getaway
14 Parade spoiler, perhaps
15 Ready to come off
16 Coloratura's piece
17 Back to being friends again?
19 Seasoned sailor
20 Ran into
21 They're sometimes fine
22 Choctaw and Chickasaw
24 St. Francis' birthplace
26 Actor James
27 Humor that doesn't cause a blush?
33 Do watercolors
36 "___ la vista"
37 Suffix with project
38 Big concert equipment
39 Skin suffixes
40 Worked-up state
41 Kelly's "___ Girls"
42 Mildew and such
43 Fountain drinks
44 Mentally sound?
47 One with an "Esq." tag
48 Zoo showoffs
52 Certain fir
55 Peak in Thessaly
57 Author Rita ___ Brown
58 Hullabaloos
59 Relapsing?
62 ___-majesté
63 Norman Vincent ___
64 More than suggest
65 Lascivious look
66 Mexicali mister
67 Batik artisan

DOWN

1 Sachet quality
2 Champs Élysées sights
3 Breaks in relations
4 Suffix with exist
5 Pastor
6 Dig like a pig
7 Written promises
8 Attendance fig., often
9 Goes back to the top
10 Pit boss's place
11 Riyadh native
12 Track event not in the Olympics
13 Praises for pups
18 Word before "a prayer" or "a clue"
23 Big Indian
25 Charged particles
26 "Far out, man!"
28 Writer with an award named after him
29 Florida's Key ___
30 Warm-hearted
31 Essayist's alias
32 6-2, 5-7, 6-3, etc.
33 ___ Alto
34 Hymn sign-off
35 ___ facto
39 They chase "bunnies"
40 Arrange logically
42 Greek cheese
43 Stiff hairs
45 Sadat's predecessor
46 Like much Jewish food
49 Manicurist's tool
50 Singer's span
51 Passover feast
52 Bouncer?
53 "Zip-___-Doo-Dah"
54 Get checkmated
55 In the blink ___ eye
56 Normandy battle site
60 License's cost
61 Nasty campaigning

by John Greenman

ACROSS

1 Bogus
6 Greeting with a smile
11 S.A.T. takers
14 Chosen ones
15 "Cry, the Beloved Country" author
16 10th-anniversary gift
17 [Hint] Apple on the head
19 Self center
20 Comparison figure
21 Lowest deck on a ship
22 Swear
23 VCR button
25 Water measurement
27 It might keep a shepherd awake
30 Pollen producer
32 Old Ford
33 Symbol of freshness
35 Kind of key
38 Come out
40 Pitch
42 The "greatest blessing" and the "greatest plague": Euripides
43 Little belittlement
45 Vaudeville dancer's prop
46 Not born yesterday
48 String decoration
50 Hiker, in a way
52 Refuse
54 Tramp's partner
55 Walpurgis Night figure
57 ___ Jones of old radio comedy
61 "You ___ here"
62 [Hint] Apple off the head
64 Annual awards giver
65 High points of a trip to South America?
66 Quartet member
67 A ship, to crew members
68 It raises dough
69 G.I. wear

DOWN

1 Sinn ___
2 What's more
3 Cordelia's father
4 Seafood dish
5 Busy person's abbr.
6 Copyists
7 Wild
8 Football legend Graham
9 Hype
10 "Barbara ___" (1966 hit)
11 [Hint] Apple in the head
12 Demanding standard
13 Buffaloes
18 Fanny Farmer treat
22 Mr. T's group
24 Slowly and evenly
26 Base
27 Squandered
28 Sphere starter
29 [Hint] Apple? Went ahead!
31 Classification
34 Superlative suffix
36 Missouri River tribe
37 Card-carrying
39 Foul
41 Image site
44 Cuddles
47 Bearish
49 Scheduled
50 Shuts (up)
51 Solid ground
53 Midsection
56 "M*A*S*H" star
58 Dissolve
59 Chili pot
60 Plug away
62 Kind of station
63 AT&T rival

by Greg Staples

ACROSS

1 Subject of a People profile
6 Hubbub
9 Father
13 Tylenol alternative
14 Temple worshiper
15 Single unit
16 Big crop in Hawaii
18 Goaded
19 End of some e-mail addresses
20 Opulence
21 Starry
22 Fix
24 Miami's ___ Bay
26 Mediocre
28 Cash register part
29 1941 Orson Welles classic
33 ___ Mahal
36 Fruity coolers
37 Note before la
38 Prefix with -nautics
39 Face off in the ring
40 Making a fuss
44 Pat Boone's "___ That a Shame"
45 Worry
46 Late prize-winning San Francisco columnist
50 Reef materials
54 Lucky charm
55 Diamond Head locale
57 Step to the plate
58 San Francisco footballer, briefly
59 Popular painkiller
61 Woman's lip application
62 "Feliz ___ nuevo"
63 Door swinger
64 E-mailed
65 Bench with a back
66 Law's partner

DOWN

1 One checking out a place in planning a crime
2 Escape the clutches of
3 Starting advantage
4 One of the Gabor sisters
5 "Symphonie fantastique" composer
6 "Stronger than dirt" sloganeer
7 Star in Cygnus
8 Have debts
9 Yahoo! or Lycos, e.g.
10 Furious
11 Song of triumph
12 Flummox
15 Biceps or triceps
17 Unlucky charm
21 "Q ___ queen"
23 Sale sign
25 Like slanted type
27 Kind of inspection
29 Taxi
30 Wedding vow
31 Cowboy's moniker
32 Some ring outcomes, for short
33 4:00 affair
34 Mr. Onassis
35 Music's ___ Bon Jovi
38 Tennis whiz
40 Kitchen gizmos
41 Med. school course
42 Cheesy snack
43 The mustachioed brother
44 Most skilled
46 Puts up, as a painting
47 Novelist Zola
48 Talk nonstop
49 Nary a soul
51 In ___ (trapped)
52 Oscar-winning Jessica
53 Navigate
56 Confess
59 Get a little shuteye
60 Tire filler

by David J. Kahn

ACROSS

1 Hula skirt material
6 Arafat's grp.
9 It may be secondhand
14 Moses' mountain
15 Varnish ingredient
16 Downy duck
17 Befuddle
18 Not cutting
20 Woman who's not very sharp?
22 Mad magazine's genre
25 Paint can direction
26 Addis Ababa's land: Abbr.
27 Mad. ___
29 Clip out
34 Chowed down
35 Stately shader
37 Every 9-Down has one
38 Girl who's got her facts wrong?
43 "Star Trek" extra
44 Cobbler
45 Windup
46 More spiteful
49 Chem. pollutant
51 Canonized Mlle.
52 New Mexico art center
54 The "N" in "N×P"
56 Man who's annually in the doghouse?
60 Aspirin target, maybe
61 Propelled a boat
65 The Little Mermaid
66 Coffee vessel
67 Extremist
68 Lavatory sign
69 Lipton product
70 Attack ad, maybe

DOWN

1 Govt. property org.
2 Purge
3 &
4 Pheasant ragout
5 ___ Nevada
6 Surveyor's map
7 Plasterwork backers
8 Fair-sized musical groups
9 Managua miss
10 Longish dress
11 Thor's father
12 Clark of the Daily Planet
13 Work unit
19 Cast-of-thousands film
21 Early evening
22 Chantey singer
23 Number one Hun
24 Grad student's work
28 Polar worker
30 Watch the kids
31 Most artful
32 Tooth: Prefix
33 Give, as an apology
36 Unruly locks
39 Harden
40 Hanky embroidery
41 Saw along the grain
42 City non-Muslims may not enter
47 Man addressed as "My Lord"
48 Cheap liquor
50 Louisiana waterways
53 English place name suffix
55 Poem of King David
56 Insignificant
57 Totally botch
58 Baseball's Saberhagen
59 Comedian Carvey
60 Henpeck
62 Rd. or hwy.
63 Unit of geologic time
64 Patriotic org.

by Cynthia Joy Higgins

ACROSS

1 Nickname for 14-Down
7 His, in France
10 School of whales
13 Like a portion of some people's income
14 Plug, of a sort
15 It may be reached by tunnel
16 Cafeteria-goers
17 Hectorer of Zeus
18 Giant of old
19 Negative particle
20 Charlie's little sister
21 Game piece
22 Stethoscope user
23 ___'acte
25 Test pilot Chuck
27 In a sad way
29 School basics, in a way
30 "Wishing Will Make ___"
33 Chicken ___
34 Michael of R.E.M.
37 Anatomical holders
38 "Entry of Christ Into Brussels" artist
40 Tumbled
41 Bor-r-r-r-ring
43 Laborer of old
44 Subjects of a U.S. Air Force cover-up?
45 Messenger ___
46 Actress Claudia
48 Some trick-or-treaters
51 Command spot
52 Dance step
55 "Norma ___"
56 Boy with a blanket
58 Peanuts, in a manner of speaking
60 Furthermore
61 List ender
62 Not blatant
63 One who might be interested in big bucks

64 ___ bath (therapeutic treatment)
65 Ran on
66 What Marcie called 52-Down
67 ___-cone
68 Impatient agreement, maybe

DOWN

1 Place
2 32-Down's was a toy
3 Place for a chest
4 Stat start
5 Bit of truth?
6 QB's gains
7 Cartoonist Silverstein
8 At dawn
9 Marathon dancers, e.g.
10 Comment from Charlie Brown
11 Musical Shaw
12 Olympics length
14 This puzzle's honoree
20 Ms. magazine co-founder
24 Microwave
26 Dexterous
27 Ship officers
28 Actress De Carlo and others
30 Suffix akin to - esque
31 Chinese truth
32 Big Beethoven devotee
35 Mideast grp.
36 Chicago trains
39 It might give you a line
42 Like a bare floor

47 "Yeah, right!"
48 Alums
49 Capital west of Haiphong
50 Protest
52 Peppermint ___
53 Tree-lined walk
54 They're pulled uphill
57 Like some peacekeepers
59 New corp. hires
62 Plant, perhaps

by Jim Page

ACROSS

1 Worker protection org.
5 Nuclear weapon
10 Cry from a crib
14 Smart-___
15 Rome's river
16 Eclipse, maybe, to the ancients
17 Shuttle launch sound
18 Verdi work
19 The African Queen, e.g.
20 1967 Van Morrison hit
23 Lose, as skin
24 "Erie Canal" mule
25 "___ la vista!"
28 The U.S.A.'s "uncle"
31 City west of Montgomery
35 Rooms with stairs leading to them
37 "Skip to My ___"
39 China's Chou En-___
40 Flowers given to the Preakness Stakes winner
44 Place with microscopes
45 14, in old Rome
46 Nail polish
47 Liability's opposite
50 Unused
52 Swap
53 Jabber
55 Reagan's first Secretary of State
57 1970 hit by Sugarloaf
63 Bring to 212 degrees
64 Charlie Chan portrayer Warner ___
65 Ooze
67 "Just this ___ . . ."
68 Recoil in pain
69 Close tightly
70 Shade of red
71 In the buff
72 Grand Ole ___

DOWN

1 Dinghy propeller
2 One whose business isn't picking up?
3 Listen to
4 Word puzzle
5 United (with)
6 Humans, e.g.
7 Listen to
8 A ___ pittance
9 Slender nails
10 Ceiling-hung art
11 Love, Spanish-style
12 Lunch or dinner
13 Aardvark's tidbit
21 Hit with a bang
22 Car fill-up
25 "Usted ___ español?"
26 Map site
27 Knife wounds
29 Tylenol competitor
30 Up-to-date
32 Incan transport
33 Like a horse or lion
34 Bridal path
36 Reason for an X rating
38 Put to work
41 Yang's counterpart
42 Before
43 ___ Sea, in the North Atlantic
48 Hole for a lace
49 Menlo Park monogram
51 From what place?
54 On the map
56 Threw in
57 Auctioneer's last word
58 Paddy crop
59 Director Kazan
60 U.S. soldier in W.W. II
61 Not shallow
62 Four seasons
63 Go up and down in the water
66 Thickness

by Gregory E. Paul

44

ACROSS

1 Current units
5 Many comedy teams
9 Squirrel away
14 Some is junk
15 Archer of "Patriot Games"
16 Marseille menu
17 Collection in Old Icelandic
18 Carpe __
19 "The __ Incident" (1943 Fonda film)
20 Assume what's being asked
23 Parting word
24 Not happy
25 Flushed
27 Trinity member
28 Ginnie __
30 Mystery writer Josephine
31 Mr. Potato Head part
32 Early Microsoft offering
33 "A mouse!"
34 Captures
35 Wake sleeping dogs, so to speak
39 __ Jones's locker
40 NASDAQ listings: Abbr.
41 Speakers' pause fillers
42 Ending with methyl
43 Round Table title
44 Indy 500 logo
45 Place to take a cure
48 Cone bearer
49 Italian poet Torquato __
51 Suffer a loss, slangily
53 Get closer to home, in a way
56 Not level
57 Like service station rags
58 Black-and-white hunter
59 __ fatale
60 At liberty
61 Victory signs
62 Long lock
63 A.T.F. agents
64 To be, to Tiberius

DOWN

1 One-celled pond dwellers
2 Got by
3 Hardly the Queen's English
4 List of candidates
5 Miami-__ County
6 More than unusual
7 Get the better of
8 Academic term
9 Shipmate of Bones and Spock
10 Downtown cruiser
11 Like sloths and tree toads
12 Alley Oop's time
13 Chop down
21 Sitcom material
22 Search for
26 Welby and Kildare: Abbr.
29 Not gregarious
32 Like some martinis
33 Sci-fi visitors
34 Air rifle ammo
35 Item that may be slid down
36 Paycheck booster
37 Least fortunate
38 Called balls and strikes
39 Rock's __ Leppard
43 The contiguous 48
44 Dirty
45 Oddballs may draw them
46 Zodiac fishes
47 "Ten-hut!" undoer
50 Talia of "Rocky"
52 Beyond's partner
54 "Desire Under the __"
55 Cereal grasses
56 Toward the tiller

by Nick Grivas

ACROSS

1 It's in a jamb
5 Schoolmarmish
9 Outback Bowl city
14 To boot
15 NBC host
16 N.B.A. star called "The Shack"
17 Stout ingredient
18 Regarding
19 Hardly cutting-edge
20 Computer business?
22 Bit of color
23 Guitarist Paul
24 Sipping specialist
25 Rifle attachment
29 Show place
32 NATO members
34 Nature of cyberspace?
39 Wash out
40 Center
42 Suffix with buck
43 Combining on the Internet?
45 Risk
47 Synthetic fiber
49 Tetra- plus one
50 Say
54 Bolivian bear
56 Chili rating unit?
57 What makes people write LOL?
63 Christina Applegate sitcom
64 Litter's littlest
65 Name that rings a bell?
66 Writer Chekhov
67 Manger visitors
68 Sitar music
69 Doesn't possess
70 Gulf of __, off the coast of Yemen
71 Feel sure about

DOWN

1 Woman of rank
2 Haakon's royal successor
3 2-Down's capital
4 Univ. marchers
5 Part of a service
6 Put up a fight
7 Division word
8 Phobos, to Mars
9 Mexicali munchie
10 Opposition
11 Had in mind
12 Satchel in Cooperstown
13 Birch relative
21 Sheltered, at sea
24 Kind of serum
25 Cracker's target
26 Symbol of happiness
27 Ye follower
28 Place for a shore dinner
30 Alternative to a fence
31 Binet data
33 Brat's look
35 Take it easy
36 Qum home
37 Reason for a suit
38 Skywalker's mentor
41 Roadside stop
44 Piece of clothing
46 Each
48 Lizard's locale?
50 Indian chief
51 "Maria __" (old tune)
52 Brig's pair
53 Gasoline may make it go
55 Protest of a sort
57 Witty Bombeck
58 Campus area
59 Picnic spot
60 Russian Everyman
61 Canceled, to NASA
62 Nibble away

by Richard Silvestri

ACROSS

1 Linemen's protectors
5 Light-refracting crystal
10 Marries
14 Coward in "The Wizard of Oz"
15 Author Bret
16 Like slanted type: Abbr.
17 The New Yorker cartoonist Peter
18 __ a time (individually)
19 Kind of wrestling
20 Buddhist discipline
21 Soul singer from California?
23 Slowly, to a conductor
25 Bullfight bull
26 California prison
29 Big airplane engine
33 Lustrous gems
35 Levi's material
37 Coronado's gold
38 Prayer opener
39 Kind of boom
40 Fake
41 Greyhound, e.g.
42 Heard, but not seen
43 Intelligence
44 Old-time Japanese governor
46 Tried and true
48 "What are the __?"
50 St. Petersburg's Hermitage, e.g.
53 Pop singer from Texas?
58 Wizards and Magic org.
59 Grad
60 Mt. Everest locale
61 "__ calling"
62 Italian money
63 Jalopy

64 Darjeeling and oolong
65 Hit the runway
66 Snake shapes
67 Johnson of "Laugh-In"

DOWN

1 Public square
2 On TV
3 Country singer from North Dakota?
4 __-Cat (off-road vehicle)
5 Snaps
6 Indian princess
7 Infuriates
8 Get the ball rolling
9 Momentarily dazzling
10 Opposite of ignorance
11 Sewing case

12 Cousin of "Phooey!"
13 Wade (through)
21 Works at the Louvre
22 Short drink
24 Olympian's quest
27 Nose tickler
28 __ Work (road repair sign)
30 Folk-rock singer from Colorado?
31 Great times
32 Scholarly book
33 Cutlass or Eighty Eight
34 "Tush!"
36 Christie's "Death on the __"
39 Big film festival name
40 Envisages
42 Autobahn car

43 Flabbergast
45 Became angry
47 Beams
49 Litigants
51 German sub
52 Parsonage
53 __ Mall (London street)
54 Inter __
55 Become a traitor
56 They'll get you in hot water
57 Noted gallery
61 __ loss for words

by Dave and Diane Epperson

ACROSS

1 Atty.-to-be's exam
5 Edith who sang "La Vie en Rose"
9 Key of Mozart's Symphony No. 39
14 Court records
15 Stewpot
16 Said à la the Raven
17 Feature of some shirts
19 "I give!"
20 "Seinfeld" miss
21 Bite, as the heels
23 Crisscross pattern
25 Catch in the act
26 Big goon
29 Decade divs.
30 "Minnie the Moocher" singer
33 See 13-Down
34 "Gil Blas" writer
35 Neuter
38 "Not ___ bet!"
40 Alkaline solutions
41 Help run, as a party
44 Part of WASP
47 Qatar, for one
49 Cone bearer
52 Fighter in gray
53 Biddy
54 Fish in a can
56 Part of a TV feed
58 "The Devil's Dictionary" author
59 In any respect
62 Baltimore chef's specialty
64 Kindled anew
65 Roof projection
66 Get out of bed
67 Intense media campaign
68 Amscrayed
69 Tolkien tree creatures

DOWN

1 In recent days
2 Like some variables
3 Times up
4 Unspoken
5 Malodorous animal
6 Needing hospital care
7 Astronaut Shepard
8 Hot breakfast dish
9 Steady
10 "Candid Camera" man
11 ___ cit. (footnote abbr.)
12 U.S./U.K. divider
13 With 33-Across, Montreal's subway
18 In a state of abeyance
22 Heavy sheet
24 River of Aragón
26 On vacation
27 Web designer's creation
28 Baby blues
31 Sir Arthur ___ Doyle
32 Capital on a fjord
33 "Butt out!," initially
35 Surgery result
36 Dermal opening
37 Ishmael's captain
39 Tiny colonists
42 Klink's aide in "Hogan's Heroes"
43 Two-___ sloth
45 Got one's mitts on
46 Ira Gershwin's contribution
48 Social welfare org.
49 Quarter-barrel
50 Theme of "Oedipus Rex"
51 ___ Pieces
55 "The Wreck of the Mary ___"
56 Touched down
57 Like some vaccines
59 Wall St. whiz
60 Bus. card abbr.
61 ___ Baba
63 Caesar's hello

by Fred Piscop

ACROSS

1 Fusses
5 Clairvoyant's claim
8 Functioning
14 OUTFIELDER
15 Chowed down
16 Projectionist's target
17 SECOND BASEMAN
19 Did a bootblacks's job
20 Jotting down
22 Start of the 18th century
23 Baseball stat
26 "Wait a ___!"
27 "___ tu" (Verdi aria)
29 Donna Shalala's dept.
30 Arafat of the P.L.O.
32 Courtroom V.I.P.
34 With 42-Across, what the 10 answers to the capitalized clues comprise
38 Literary adverb
39 Mr. Onassis, familiarly
40 Harem rooms
42 See 34-Across
47 Posts
48 Priced to move
49 Draft org.
52 As well
53 United Nations Day mo.
54 Acid
55 What the fat lady sings?
57 SHORTSTOP
60 "___ ergo sum"
62 OUTFIELDER
66 LEFT-HANDED PITCHER
67 Actress Sue ___ Langdon
68 OUTFIELDER
69 Like some inclement weather
70 Go down
71 Opportunity

DOWN

1 Airport abbr.
2 Twosome
3 Handicapper's place: Abbr.
4 Tibia
5 New York's time zone
6 Zeno, for one
7 Ivy League school, briefly
8 ___ Enterprise
9 THIRD BASEMAN
10 Parched
11 CATCHER
12 Moocher
13 "The ___ near!"
18 ___-um (gnat)
21 FIRST BASEMAN
23 RIGHT-HANDED PITCHER
24 Cotton bundles
25 ___ of Langerhans
28 King, in Cádiz
31 Beat it
32 Goes bad
33 Almost an eternity
35 One who hems, but doesn't haw
36 "Let's Make ___"
37 Heavy hammers
41 Went like a leadfoot
43 Knocking sound
44 Spanish uncle
45 Small curl of hair
46 Pentium processor maker
49 Punches
50 Wind up
51 Musical transition
53 Put one's two cents in
56 Abundant
58 "___ a Teen-age Werewolf"
59 Steals, old-style
61 ___-10 (acne-fighting medicine)
63 Sound of delight
64 Muscle: Prefix
65 Fast wings

by Peter Gordon

ACROSS

1 Pinball message
5 Saloon orders
9 "A Lesson From ___"
14 Soprano's song, maybe
15 Nod off
16 One of the senses
17 Hiker's woe
18 Colorado skiing destination
19 Follow
20 Intermittently
23 A single time
24 "___ it or lose it"
25 Frequently, to Shakespeare
28 Exterminator's target
31 Nod off
34 Arc de Triomphe locale
36 Mexican gold
37 "Livin' la Vida ___" (Ricky Martin song)
38 Intermittently
42 Surf's sound
43 Shipment to a mill
44 Rephrases
45 Guggenheim display
46 Brand-new business
49 Nintendo product
50 Expire
51 Lennon's in-laws
53 Intermittently
61 Sailors are famous for them
62 Fur, say
63 Down-to-earth
64 Pal
65 Excited about
66 Food for Fido
67 Reveal
68 Like a billionaire's pockets
69 Wall Street inits.

DOWN

1 Word before shell or Bell
2 Remove the wrinkles from
3 Peseta : Spain :: ___ : Italy
4 Argentine dance
5 Reply from Ann Landers
6 Repair shop substitute
7 Basso Pinza
8 The first "S" in S.A.S.E.
9 "Relax, soldier!"
10 Jessica of "Tootsie"
11 Bones, to a doctor
12 Pins and needles holder
13 Spotted
21 On pins and needles
22 Fold-up mattress
25 Where to hear a 14-Across
26 Party handout
27 "Trick or ___"
29 Necessity at a golf club
30 George Gershwin's brother
31 Like a pitcher's perfect game
32 Vinegar: Prefix
33 Colorful violet
35 Abbr. on sale items
37 Inc., in Britain
39 Jottings
40 "... man ___ mouse?"
41 Train station
46 Squelches
47 Until now
48 Remove a clog from
50 Muralist Rivera
52 Kitchen wrap
53 Slanted type: Abbr.
54 Identify
55 Fly like a butterfly
56 Amino, for one
57 Second to ___
58 Bank (on)
59 Memorial Day solo
60 ___ gin fizz

by Gregory E. Paul

ACROSS

1 Sixth sense
4 Sprightly dances
8 Egypt's Sadat
13 Designer Cassini
15 Taj Mahal site
16 Bellini opera
17 Caretaker for a baby
18 Sticky stuff
19 Gnawed
20 Austrian observance of April 30
23 Meadow
24 Like wind chimes
25 British observance of April 23
31 Onetime Argentine leader
32 ___ Perot
33 How to address a Fr. lady
36 The Emerald Isle
37 Airport abbr.
38 Ukraine's capital
39 Prevail
40 Fisher's rental
42 Stretched tight
43 Indian observance of April 13
45 Connecting strips of land
48 Trivial Pursuit need
49 United States observance of April 14
55 Perform penance
56 Evictee from paradise
57 ___ Bator
59 Deluxe sheet material
60 One-liner, e.g.
61 Aggregate
62 Golf great Sam

63 Stout relatives
64 Mack or Danson

DOWN

1 Ages and ages
2 Order at KFC
3 Pitcher Alejandro
4 Black-spotted cat
5 Composer Stravinsky
6 Seaman's quaff
7 H. H. Munro's pseudonym
8 Biblical liar
9 Zilch
10 Jalopy
11 Menotti hero
12 Worn-out
14 Old fighting vessel
21 Lowly worker
22 Rules: Abbr.

25 Gush forth
26 Hatcher of "Lois & Clark"
27 Happy face
28 Accra's land
29 Bobble
30 Newswoman Tabitha
33 Warship danger
34 Tableland
35 At any time
38 Excited
40 Praise
41 "I cannot tell ___"
42 Double
43 Grammy-winning Twain
44 "My Cup Runneth Over" singer, 1967
45 Bridge declaration

46 Beelzebub
47 Savings vehicle, briefly
50 Punjabi prince
51 Screen fave
52 Bake sale order
53 Came to rest
54 New Haven school
58 Composer Rorem

by D. J. DeChristopher

ACROSS

1 Nurse's item
5 Some change
10 "The Far Pavilions" author M. M. ___
14 Worrying words from a driver
15 Campaign stop, e.g.
16 "Shoo!"
17 St. Bernard sound
18 "Cheers" barmaid
19 Little dog, for short
20 1936 film starring 57-Across
23 Row
24 1934 film starring 57-Across
28 Compass line
31 Treated with contempt
34 Fam. member
35 1938 film starring 57-Across
37 Actress Dee
39 Target of some creams
40 Lakers' org.
42 Road shoulder
43 Many winter vacationers
46 1949 film starring 57-Across
49 Abbr. on a business letter
50 Tchotchke holder
52 NNW's opposite
53 1957 film starring 57-Across
55 Bub
57 Actor born April 5, 1900
63 Shake up
66 Ernest ___, winner of the first Pulitzer for fiction
67 Greek liqueur
68 Zone
69 Gallops
70 Stick in one's ___

71 Tough test, informally
72 Pass
73 Marx with a manifesto

DOWN

1 Farm females
2 Rider's command
3 In a few minutes
4 Like some shows
5 Actress Yvonne
6 "Terrible" one
7 Ford product, briefly
8 Sign up
9 Socks away
10 "Wham!"
11 Knock over
12 Gab
13 Electric ___
21 Air-filled item, maybe

22 Last part
25 Info for waiters
26 Kind of wheel
27 How some steak is served
28 Humiliated
29 "All-American" fellow
30 Hardly optimists
32 Have
33 Remove from a sack
36 "Understand?"
38 Measurements overseer: Abbr.
41 Drink suffix
44 Legal defendant: Abbr.
45 Church part
47 Chair part
48 Gist
51 When there's darkness, in a Koestler title

54 Relatively cool sun
56 Butter holder
58 Club of song
59 Utility abbr.
60 Emanation
61 6-Down, e.g.
62 Long, dismal cry
63 Quick punch
64 Vein pursuit
65 Flock's place

by Frances Hansen

52

ACROSS

1 Dress shirt closer
5 Four times a day, on an Rx
8 Person who doesn't put down roots
13 Had on
14 Acapulco article
15 State as one's view
16 Nitwit's swoon?
18 Nonsense, slangily
19 Torah holders
20 New York tribe defeated by the Iroquois
21 Exterior
22 Cartoon Chihuahua
23 On the house
24 Respect
25 Kind of eyes
27 Force (open)
28 Turn one way and then back
29 "A Tale ___ Cities"
30 Uncompromising sort
33 Regret some stupidity . . . with a hint to this puzzle's theme
37 Girls in the family
38 Watergate hearings chairman Sam
40 Univ. where "Good Will Hunting" is set
43 Suffix with neat or beat
44 ___ Conventions
45 Shabbily clothed
47 Rock star, e.g.
49 Speed (up)
50 Vinegar: Prefix
51 Pre-remote channel changer
52 R.E.M.'s "It's the End of the World ___ Know It"
53 Danger in dangerous waters
54 Spring in the air?
56 News groups
57 "Tastes great!"
58 "___ do for now"
59 Analyze the composition of
60 N.B.A. tiebreakers
61 Like some orders

DOWN

1 Promised to give up
2 Was attentive
3 Internet addresses
4 "Excellent!," in slang
5 Paper quantity
6 Type of 39-Down
7 Movie companion, maybe
8 Vibes not being picked up by anyone?
9 Painkiller since ancient times
10 "Uncle" of early television
11 Rages
12 Some tractors
16 Red River city
17 Houston hockey player
23 Doing credible work as a magician?
24 Mozart's "Madamina," e.g.
26 Verdon of "Damn Yankees"
27 Top exec.
30 Miner's tool
31 Hawaiian instrument, for short
32 Pulled apart
34 Gifts at Honolulu Airport
35 Push too hard, as an argument
36 Have it good
39 Belly part
40 Bad atmosphere
41 "
42 Steps (on)
44 Asian desert
46 Places in the heart
47 Contribution, as of ideas
48 Buildings near some cafeterias
51 Bout-ending slug
52 Mennen shaving brand
55 Shining

by Manny Nosowsky

Turn the completed grid into a greeting card!

ACROSS

1 Indian music
5 12-time Pro Bowl pick Junior ___
9 N.F.L. game divs.
13 Close to closed
14 In debt
15 Europe/Asia boundary river
16 Step 1: Highlight this answer
19 Strainer
20 Sailor's "Stop!"
21 Wharf workers' org.
24 Little Rock-to-Birmingham dir.
25 Demolish
27 Step 2: With 43-and 55-Across, do this in the grid (scrambled or not) . . . it works for almost anyone!
33 How Santa dresses, mostly
34 Saturday worshipers
35 Electrical law maker
36 Diamond of note
37 Build ___ (settle down)
39 Canadian native
40 Fellow, in British slang
41 Co. figure
42 Belfry sound
43 See 27-Across
47 With 48-Across, ". . . and that ___!"
48 See 47-Across
49 End of a machine gun sound
50 "Star Wars" title
53 The heart in "I Love New York" signs, e.g.
55 See 27-Across
61 Big name in supercomputers
62 Set one's sights on
63 Sleep symbols

64 Prime coffee-growing area in Hawaii
65 Ferris wheel site
66 North Sea feeder

DOWN

1 Good cheer?
2 Steely Dan's best-selling album
3 Feature of Alfred E. Neuman's smile
4 Some Dada prints
5 Feature of many an office chair
6 Green land
7 Figure on a hill
8 Cry before or after sticking out the tongue
9 Eighth note
10 "___ Little Tenderness" (1960s hit)

11 "Darn it all!"
12 Part of a schedule
14 Overly large
17 End-of-ramp directive
18 Stuns
21 Bakers' coats
22 A suspect might appear in one
23 Make it
25 Sts. and rds.
26 Periodic table no.
28 Framable frame
29 Bounce
30 Irritated with
31 Louise's cinematic partner
32 Western ___
37 Nerve appendage
38 Like "das" in Ger.
39 King's employer

41 Root who won the 1912 Nobel Peace Prize
42 Excite
44 One of the Jacksons
45 1977 James Brolin thriller with the tagline "What EVIL drives . . ."
46 Usually black garb
50 Where to tie one on?
51 Rounded hairdo
52 Meg of "You've Got Mail"
53 Do followers
54 Tag info
56 Part of Britain's mil.
57 Estuary
58 Reef dweller
59 Grain Belt state: Abbr.
60 "The Waste Land" poet's monogram

by Patrick Merrell

ACROSS
1 See 48-Down
5 Stick in one's ___
9 Frank of the Mothers of Invention
14 Not loco
15 "___ and the King of Siam"
16 Decorate
17 Bess Truman or Barbara Bush
19 Snooped, with "about"
20 "You're ___ talk!"
21 Enclosure with a MS.
23 NNW's opposite
24 Hi-___ monitor
25 Question after the fact
29 Car bomb?
31 Old letter salutation
32 "God's Little ___" (Erskine Caldwell best seller)
34 Competitor of Dove or Camay
36 Prop for Picasso
40 Takes care of all possibilities
44 Pan-cooked brunch treat
45 Words after "... as long as you both shall live?"
46 "Mona ___"
47 Make the cut?
50 Funny DeGeneres
52 Grilling
56 "Shame on you!"
59 Crew's control?
60 One who indulges too much in the grape
61 French city famous for its mustard
63 Garbo of "Mata Hari," 1932
65 1990 Macaulay Culkin film
68 Ed of "Lou Grant"
69 The "U" in B.T.U.
70 Compete in the America's Cup
71 Bookcase part

72 Model Banks
73 Med school subj.

DOWN
1 In regard to
2 Where Bangor is
3 Put aside for later
4 Place for eggs
5 Iron Man Ripken of the Orioles
6 Genetic letters
7 ___ forth (et cetera)
8 Brother comic Shawn or Marlon
9 "Riders of the Purple Sage" author
10 Hullabaloo
11 Star's entourage
12 "... or ___ 1 for more options"
13 Peruvian peaks
18 Play with, as a Frisbee
22 Star Wars program, for short

26 Morays, e.g.
27 Hint
28 Fit to be tried?
30 More profound
32 U.N.C.'s athletic org.
33 Where streets intersect: Abbr.
35 "Sweet" age in ancient Rome?
37 Play by George Bernard Shaw
38 Superman's symbol
39 Meadow
41 Relatively low-temperature star
42 German river in a 1943 R.A.F. raid
43 Part to play
48 With 1-Across, infamous Ugandan dictator
49 Opposite of "At ease!"

51 Mother of Castor and Pollux
52 "Animal House" party costumes
53 Like winters in the Arctic
54 Ballroom dancer Castle
55 Foolish person, slangily
57 Braga of "Kiss of the Spider Woman"
58 Prepared to pray
62 She requested "As Time Goes By"
64 ___ Aviv
66 Bygone Russian space station
67 When a plane is due in: Abbr.

by Randall J. Hartman

ACROSS

1 Kaplan of "Welcome Back, Kotter"
5 Tally
10 Émile who wrote "Truth is on the march"
14 Is in hock
15 More than sore
16 Leave out
17 Ronald Reagan movie
20 Think tank products
21 Indy 500 inits.
22 Cuban boy in 2000 news
23 As a result
25 Chat room shorthand for "Here's what I think"
27 "Rule, Britannia" composer
30 Doris Day movie, with "The"
35 ___ Paulo, Brazil
36 Era-spanning story
37 Greg of "My Two Dads"
38 Honda with a palindromic name
40 Gradual decline
42 Cause of some food poisoning
43 2001 title role for Audrey Tautou
45 Wren or hen
47 ___ Irvin, longtime cartoonist for The New Yorker
48 Rock Hudson movie
50 Not fem.
51 Deuce beater
52 Bonkers
54 "___ is human"
57 Sandy island
59 Football's Fighting ___
63 Barbara Eden TV series
66 ___ St. Vincent Millay
67 Old newspaper sections
68 Touch-and-go

69 Support staffer: Abbr.
70 Map detail
71 Have-___ (lower economic group)

DOWN

1 Mongolian expanse
2 Impressed and then some
3 "Venerable" monk
4 Bequeathed property
5 Colgate competitor
6 Equestrian competition
7 Bonkers
8 A world without 71-Across
9 According to
10 Of the animal kingdom
11 First Dodge with front-wheel drive

12 Minnelli of "Arthur"
13 Like ___ of bricks
18 Suffix with bull or bear
19 Didn't act up
24 Work ___ lather
26 Flaubert's Bovary, e.g.: Abbr.
27 B.M.I. rival
28 "Spider-Man" director Sam
29 It's no short story
31 ___ the Hutt of "Star Wars"
32 Ancient meeting place
33 Maxim's target audience
34 Pioneering 1940s computer
36 Annabella of "The Sopranos"
39 "It's on me!"

41 Subject of a 1976 film "ode"
44 Stand-in for "you" in "Concentration"
46 "Flying Down to Rio" studio
49 Captain of industry
50 Informal greeting at a breakfast shop
53 Grp. known as the Company
54 "___ yellow ribbon . . ."
55 Bookie's quote
56 Coastal raptors
58 P.M. periods
60 Dope
61 Sort (through)
62 Attention getters
64 Hosp. procedure
65 Ballpark fig.

by Dave Mackey

ACROSS

1 "The Divine Comedy," for one
5 Elisabeth of "Cocktail"
9 Housecat
14 It could be revolving
15 Mann of the Haus
16 High-end Honda
17 Windsor princess
18 Book of Mormon book
19 Dizzy Gillespie's jazz
20 "I asked for tomato bisque, not gazpacho!" (complaint #1)
23 Place for a housecat
24 ___ du Diable
25 Cousin of "aargh!"
28 "Has our waiter even made eye contact?" (complaint #2)
33 ___-Magnon
34 Shad ___
35 Sharpshooting Annie
36 Chart anew
39 14+
41 Zig and zag
42 Money for money
44 Au naturel
46 Something Elizabeth II has?
47 "What, are they growing the food?" (complaint #3)
51 Sevilla seasoning
52 Manhandle
53 Actor Stephen
54 Title of this puzzle
60 Place for a barbecue
63 Titan's place
64 A rock band's name often appears on it
65 Bikini, e.g.
66 Language of the Hindustan Express
67 Sci-fi sage
68 Al ___ (a bit firm)
69 Mulching material
70 10 C-notes

DOWN

1 Mild yellow cheese
2 My Little ___ (kids' toy line)
3 Charge holders
4 Spicy cuisine
5 Free local paper
6 Prefix with sphere
7 Mantel pieces
8 13th-century king of Denmark
9 Workshop fixture
10 Nailed, as a test
11 Pal
12 Pal
13 Pie hole
21 Motor City org.
22 Mishmash
25 On fire
26 Ingenious
27 Excited, with "up"
28 Queen of Soul, familiarly
29 German commander at the invasion of Normandy
30 Marker
31 ___ jacket
32 "South Park" boy
33 Sticking points?
37 It has a horn: Abbr.
38 Apartment security feature
40 Distant
43 Morales of "La Bamba"
45 Long past its prime
48 Confesses (to)
49 Bloodshot
50 Pops
54 Suffer from the heat
55 The Old Sod
56 Robert who won a Tony for "Guys and Dolls"
57 Fairway club
58 Like Michelangelo's David
59 Webzine
60 Crash site?
61 Had a bit
62 Won ___

by Daniel Kantor and Jay Kaskel

ACROSS

1 Vampire's tooth
5 Playing marble
10 At any time
14 Pi r squared, for a circle
15 Engine
16 Lucy Lawless TV role
17 From ___ (completely)
18 Cheri formerly of "S.N.L."
19 Persia, today
20 Bidding impediment?
23 "Ooh, tasty!"
26 Enter
27 Streisand film about a Jewish girl masquerading as a boy
28 How sardines may be packed
30 Suffix with vocal
32 Enzyme suffix
33 Outdoor meal deterrent?
38 Gas brand with the slogan "Put a tiger in your tank"
39 Book after Daniel
40 Show ___ (attend, as a meeting)
44 Truth obstruction?
47 ___ Francisco
50 Inc., abroad
51 Lawn care brand
52 Garbage
54 Tipplers
57 The second "S" in MS-DOS: Abbr.
58 Metallic element's obstacle?
62 Small plateau
63 Singer Bryant
64 January to December
68 Humdinger
69 Odometer units
70 Nautilus captain
71 Chair or pew
72 Happening
73 Photo often taken after an accident

DOWN

1 Air safety org.
2 Murals and such
3 Opposite of paleo-
4 Mideast's ___ Strip
5 BP gas brand
6 Crime boss known as the Teflon Don
7 Had dinner at home
8 Bullring bull
9 "___ go bragh!"
10 Napoleon, on Elba or St. Helena
11 "The Two Gentlemen of ___"
12 Passes, as a law
13 Annoy
21 Aptly named tropical fruit
22 Computer memory unit
23 "Eek!"
24 Les États-___
25 Beaded shoes, informally
29 "Are you ___ out?"
30 "___ a man with seven wives"
31 Neuter
34 Casual conversation
35 Wrestling move
36 "___ live and breathe!"
37 German industrial valley
41 No ___ allowed (sign)
42 Hurting all over
43 Some boxing results
45 Grades 1 to 12, briefly
46 Mozart's "___ Fan Tutte"
47 Actor John of "Full House"
48 Dahl or Francis
49 Pregnancy symptom, frequently
53 Brainy
54 Photographer's request
55 Frequently
56 "Here's mud in your eye!," e.g.
59 Partner of rank and serial number
60 Prof's place: Abbr.
61 Wildcat
65 Suffix with musket
66 Doc's org.
67 Dodgers catcher Campanella

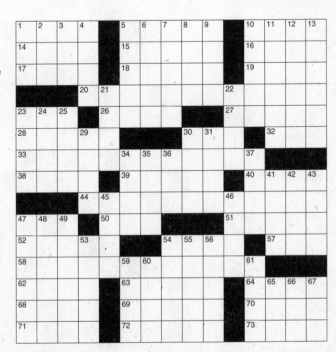

by Christina Houlihan Kelly

ACROSS

1 Like a cold fish
6 Final Four games
11 Item in a bucket
14 Lash ___ of old westerns
15 Bring shame to
16 Greeting at the Forum
17 *Myopic cartoon fellow
19 Drink from a snifter, e.g.
20 Garbage hauler
21 Rowlands of "Gloria"
22 Charlie of the Stones
24 Film terrier
26 Victoria Falls river
28 Fess up to
31 Boots, gloves, mask, etc.
33 Took off excess pounds
35 ___ huff
36 One way to run
39 Muesli morsel
40 Kind of exam, with a hint to the answers to the four starred clues
43 U2's home: Abbr.
44 Inuit's transport
46 Born, in France
47 Former Disney chief Michael
49 Home of the Scarlet Knights
52 Dangerous gas
53 Soft, colorful candy
55 "___ Flux" (Charlize Theron film)
57 Clear the blackboard
58 ___ de vie (brandies)
60 What icicles do
64 Japanese band

65 *Popular tune around Halloween
68 June honoree
69 "Golden" tune
70 Gave a beating to
71 U.S.N.A. grad: Abbr.
72 Chills out
73 Start-up costs, of sorts

DOWN

1 Beggar's cry
2 Not of the clergy
3 Approximately
4 Be more patient than
5 Agent's take
6 Just like
7 Israel's Abba
8 16 or Seventeen
9 Prefix with bar
10 "Prove it!"

11 *Plan hatcher
12 Former Disney chief Michael
13 Soda selection
18 Mil. unit
23 Simple rhyme scheme
25 ___ cell research
27 On top of things
28 Big deals
29 Call up
30 *Some ticket issuers
32 Passer of bad checks
34 Dog from Down Under
37 Treat that's sometimes dunked
38 "Show Boat" composer
41 Diving board locales
42 Muralist Joan

45 Clothes, informally
48 Sleep inducer of song
50 Richter scale blip
51 Pan-fries
53 Crystal-lined rock
54 Word before blight or sprawl
56 Program file extension
59 "___ stands . . ."
61 Angry outburst
62 "It makes sense to me"
63 Advanced degs.
66 Soccer stadium shout
67 ___ Dome (Colts' longtime home)

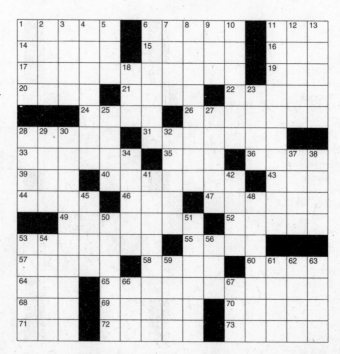

by Ken Bessette

ACROSS

1 Movement branded as "anti-art"
5 Causing ruin
10 In a frenzy
14 They can be inflated
15 Vacuous
16 Volcanic output
17 INK
20 "___ to Joy"
21 Vetoes
22 Part of a chamber orchestra
23 River in a 1957 hit film
24 Neither's partner
25 IN
33 Welcome forecast
34 Baby bottom cleaner
35 Itinerary word
36 Mentions further
37 Marshmallow candies in Easter baskets
39 Trap buildup
40 "Mamma ___!"
41 Knitter's stitch
42 Shot with lots of English
43 I
47 Panel layer
48 Hound's quarry
49 A G8 nation
52 "Well done!"
54 Family nickname
57 -
60 Fraternal group
61 Finger, in a way
62 Tyrannical sort
63 Go well together
64 Recorder function
65 "I'm glad THAT's over!"

DOWN

1 South Beach style
2 Like sharp cheddar
3 Bonehead
4 Volcanic output
5 Of a son or daughter
6 It may cause a coma
7 Bit of Watergate evidence
8 2007 y 2008, por ejemplo
9 Headed
10 Herb of A & M records
11 Clayey sediment
12 Lionel train layout, often
13 Drop for the count
18 Egypt's Sadat
19 Teatime biscuit
23 Sephia and Sportage
24 Drops off
25 Scalawag
26 Nostalgic number
27 Symbol of Lebanon
28 Belabor, with "on"
29 B.M.O.C., e.g.
30 Dispatch boat
31 Infomercial knife
32 All gone, as dinner
37 Pint-size
38 Christian ___
39 Tollbooth access
41 Coral producer
42 No-brainer?
44 Big media display
45 Ptolemy's lighthouse locale
46 Result of stream erosion
49 Footnote word
50 Game piece
51 Tests, in a way
52 Scavenger at Yellowstone
53 Pro ___
54 Sound of resignation
55 Memo phrase
56 Show unfairly
58 Historic lead-in
59 Org. that's in the red?

by Edward Sessa

ACROSS

1 Do some fall farmwork
5 Servings of corn
9 Windshield material
14 Auto shaft
15 Ladder rung
16 Actor Murphy of old westerns
17 Twelvemonth
18 Symbol of a new start
20 Low-growing tree found typically in rocky soil
22 Joined by treaty
23 Tax org.
24 Actress Longoria
25 Byways: Abbr.
26 Dangerous cargo
30 Does the butterfly, e.g.
32 Fugard's "A Lesson From ___"
33 It indicates the seconds on a clock face
37 Aussie jumpers
38 Three squares, e.g.
39 ___ Lackawanna (bygone railroad)
40 Small whirlwind
42 Carpenter's tool
43 "As You Like It" forest
44 Ransacked and robbed
45 Seer's gift, briefly
48 It's about 78% nitrogen
49 Butterfly catcher
50 Hasty glance
52 Stock transaction done at a loss for tax purposes
57 Old radio part
59 "Stronger than dirt" sloganeer
60 Commerce on the Web

61 Out of harbor
62 Visitors to baby Jesus
63 Drug-yielding shrub
64 "Hey!"
65 Once, long ago

DOWN

1 Sunbeams
2 Prez or veep
3 Banned spray on apple trees
4 Lima's land
5 Debutante's date
6 Book of maps
7 Smell horrible
8 Fat farm
9 Old-fashioned light
10 Pause
11 Red who fought oil well fires
12 Put in place
13 Does some spring farmwork
19 Forces at sea
21 Favoritism or discrimination
24 Actor Tom of "The Girl Can't Help It"
26 Difficult
27 Baseball's Felipe or Jesus
28 Places with exotic animals
29 Legendary Washington hostess Perle ___
30 Lover
31 Bookcase part
33 Cut apart
34 Asia's ___ Sea
35 Three's opposite on a clock face

36 Land owner's document
38 Steak order
41 Bram Stoker novel
42 Central part
44 Usher again
45 Roof's edge
46 Sudden outpouring
47 Pie nut
49 Local theaters, in slang
51 Go to rack and ___
52 Pantywaist
53 Unchanged
54 Not quite closed
55 Doesn't keep up
56 Number on an Interstate sign
58 Faucet

by Janet R. Bender

ACROSS

1 What a gal has that a gent doesn't?
6 Elephant of children's literature
11 Church perch
14 Correspondence sans stamp
15 Muscat resident
16 Mystifying Mr. Geller
17 Fishing trawler's haul?
19 Opposite of max.
20 Board of directors hiree
21 ___ Plaines, Ill.
22 Needed fixing, as a faucet
24 Suffix with east or west
25 Lukas of "Witness"
27 QB boo-boos: Abbr.
28 Seat of government's acquisitions?
32 Family cars
35 Whichever
36 1910s–'20s car inits.
37 Upturned, as a crate
38 Gallery display
39 Parade entry
41 Yeoman's agreement
42 Caesar of comedy
43 Big Easy team
44 Publisher's windfall?
48 Terra firma
49 Money maker
50 Celestial altar
53 Getting slick during winter
56 Funny Charlotte
57 Business owner's dreaded ink color
58 Jazz instrument
59 Salary for selling insects as food?

62 Big galoot
63 "Snowy" bird
64 Ryder rival
65 "That's a go"
66 Fakes out with fancy footwork
67 By itself

DOWN

1 Therefore
2 Mideast pooh-bah
3 Betray, in a way
4 Gambler's cube
5 Campaigner's greeting
6 Dwarf tree
7 Parisian pal
8 Wedding reception staple
9 How curses are exchanged
10 On the upswing
11 Works out with weights
12 Lake next to Avon Lake
13 Kiting necessity
18 Harvests
23 Sch. monitor
26 "American Idol" quest
28 Pink-slip
29 Industrious insect
30 Spiffy
31 Elbow-benders
32 "General Hospital," for one
33 New Age superstar
34 Throws in the trash
38 Run on TV
39 Add some meat to the bones
40 Fleur-de-___
42 Go off a diet big-time

43 Mount of the Ten Commandments
45 Forever and a day
46 Manipulated, as an election
47 Many Guinness listings
50 Loud, as a crowd
51 Twin of Romulus
52 Fred's dancing sister
53 "Look here, old chap!"
54 Part of Batman's ensemble
55 "The other white meat"
60 "Didn't I tell you?"
61 ___ Guevara

by Nancy Salomon

ACROSS

1 Low pitch symbol
6 Prepare for a physical exam
11 Upper limit
14 Where the action is
15 Not the whole thing
16 "Say what?"
17 Mercury
19 In the past
20 Wasn't quite vertical
21 Where to spend time with moguls?
23 What French fries are fried in
26 Poli ___
28 Other, in Zaragoza
29 All riled up
31 Working the desk, say
33 Listing in Hoyle's
34 Tower-top attraction
36 Bear, in Bilbao
37 Chicago-to-Pittsburgh dir.
38 Ate, but not much
40 "Bill Moyers Journal" airer
43 Hawks' and Raptors' grp.
45 Archer who aims for the heart
46 Sheriff Andy Taylor's kid
47 Part of the Kazakhstan landscape
49 Neil Simon's "Lost in ___"
51 Fine spray
52 Type measures
54 SATs
55 And so on and so forth
57 Courtier
59 Barracks boss, for short

60 Easily set off, as a temper
65 Bygone French coin
66 "I'm so bored" feeling
67 Smoked or pickled
68 Tsp. or qt.
69 Paralegals, e.g.: Abbr.
70 Oglers

DOWN

1 Help page rubric
2 Premier ___ (wine designation)
3 Grass skirt accessory
4 Hem in
5 Try to get by through bluffing
6 English
7 Pinball game stoppers

8 Gun in the garage?
9 Strands after a blizzard
10 Free use of a company car, say
11 #1 on the Hot 100
12 Prognostication
13 LP player
18 Spit
22 Notes in a pot
23 Engage
24 Big burden
25 Discoverer of stars?
27 See 30-Down
30 With 27-Down, western cry
32 Pixel
35 Wave catcher?
38 Chance
39 Weather map line
41 Word with early or whirly
42 Legis. meeting

44 "La Belle et la ___"
46 Nice enough fellow
47 Soap alternative
48 State trees of Texas
50 "I ain't buyin' it!"
51 It has a test of brightness
53 Walk proudly
56 Sister and wife of Hyperion
58 Former newspaper publisher ___ Chandler
61 Elected group
62 M.A. hopeful's test
63 Suffix with election
64 Pikes, e.g.: Abbr.

by Stephen Edward Anderson

Note: 17- and 64-Across and 11- and 34-Down each conceals an article of clothing.

ACROSS

1 "Miss America" might be printed on one
5 Mafia bosses
10 "Ali ___ and the Forty Thieves"
14 Painterish
15 Japanese cartoons
16 Grandson of Adam
17 Boardinghouse sign
19 Perched on
20 Together
21 Canceled
22 Goes out in a game of rummy
23 Katmandu resident
25 Snarled mess
27 Old-time actress Turner
29 "Chill!"
32 Many conundrums have them
35 Sneak peek: Var.
39 Suffix with human or organ
40 Pitcher's stat
41 Making out . . . or a hint to this puzzle's four hidden articles of clothing
42 4:00 drink
43 Pages that aren't editorial matter
44 Open, as an envelope
45 Pod contents
46 Perfectly clear
48 Some creepy-crawlies
50 Vinegary
54 Slave
58 The "C" in T.L.C.
60 Openly declare
62 Eskimo home
63 ___ Romeo (car)
64 Halifax's home
66 Male-only
67 El ___, Spanish artist
68 Cooking fat
69 Sharpen, as skills
70 Church council
71 God of war

DOWN

1 Brand of kitchen wrap
2 Lifted off the launch pad, e.g.
3 Not stand completely erect
4 Church songbooks
5 Purrer
6 Soon, to poets
7 Stove light
8 Letter after phi, chi, psi
9 Not vacillating about
10 Snoopy, for one
11 Favoring common folk
12 Great benefit
13 Nile reptiles
18 Emmy-winning Ward
24 Permanently, as writing
26 Tour de France winner LeMond
28 Rainbow shapes
30 Between ports
31 Lennon/Ono's "Happy ___ (War Is Over)"
32 Sound of laughter
33 Language of Lahore
34 Daytona 500 enthusiast
36 ___ out a living
37 Lab bottle
38 Not yet burning
41 Michelangelo's David, e.g.
45 Shaded passageway
47 Time of advancing glaciers
49 À la mode
51 Zesty flavors
52 Old piano key material
53 Witches' group
55 Place to exchange "I do's"
56 Valley known for its chateaux
57 Laundry units
58 Bills and coins
59 Saxophone type
61 Texas city on the Brazos
65 Old prairie home material

by Gary Disch

ACROSS

1 No stranger to the slopes
7 Bun
11 Sporty auto, for short
14 Tried one's hand (at)
15 Mongolia's home
16 Cigarette's end
17 semiautobiographical Bob Fosse film
19 Tai ___ (meditative martial art)
20 "Saturday Night Live" bit
21 Schnoz
22 Creature from the forest moon of Endor
24 Country singer Tucker
26 Blacken on the barbecue
28 Laid up
30 "Brokeback Mountain" director Lee
31 "Well, ___-di-dah!"
33 "Lord of the Rings" studio
35 River along the Quai d'Orsay
37 Highlander's textile pattern
38 A.L. M.V.P. in 2003, 2005 and 2007
41 Trumpeted
42 Things to whistle
43 New Jersey's ___ Air Force Base
45 Bogey beater
46 Certain NCO
49 "Getting close"
50 Arizona birthplace of Cesar Chavez
52 More cunning
54 It's a piece of work
56 Decisive defeat
58 Book after II Chronicles
59 Part of a coffee service
60 1970s joint U.S./Soviet space project
63 Sharp turn
64 Ilk
65 "___ Bells"
66 Suffix with modern
67 Former mates
68 Followed orders

DOWN

1 Daisy developed by Luther Burbank
2 Brand name in dog food
3 In neutral
4 Loco
5 "Yecch!"
6 Ancient land along the Dead Sea
7 Eastern prince
8 Resident of Japan's "second city"
9 Claiborne of fashion
10 Loll
11 Supporter of the House of Stuart
12 Namesake of a branch of Judaism
13 4, on a keypad
18 Modern dance music originating in Detroit
23 The Beatles' "I Am the ___"
25 Only son of Czar Nicholas II
27 Eye part
29 Cub's place
32 Hang on the line
34 Exactas and trifectas
35 Blood fluids
36 Summer hrs. along the Atlantic
38 The Rock
39 Georgia city or college
40 Drag performer with a wax likeness in New York's Madame Tussauds
41 Audi competitor
44 It was divided by the Iron Curtain
46 Alignment of the sun, earth and moon, e.g.
47 Punishing rod
48 Loco
51 Lawn diggers
53 Spaghetti western director Sergio
55 Actress Winslet
57 Hitler : Germany :: ___ : Japan
59 Gun in an action film
61 Eucharist vessel
62 Sis or bro

by Will Nediger

ACROSS

1 Taunt
5 Slalomer's moves
9 "And ___ ask is a tall ship . . .": John Masefield
13 Sans deferment
14 Till you get it right
16 "Present" in bad kids' Christmas stockings
17 Acapulco acclamations
18 Bellini two-acter
19 Fail miserably, in slang
20 1968 Glen Campbell hit
23 Daughter of Muhammad Ali
24 Cut into parts
25 Mouse who's always throwing bricks at Krazy Kat
27 Hardly stuffy
28 Aficionado
29 Gets
34 1960 Ray Charles hit
40 Peace-and-quiet venue
41 "Whaddya waitin' for?!"
42 Title lover in a 1920s Broadway hit
44 Little fingers or toes
47 He wrote "If God did not exist, it would be necessary to invent him"
52 Borrow a partner
53 1982 Willie Nelson hit
55 Nolo contendere, for one
56 Get by
57 False deity
58 "Gilmore Girls" daughter
59 New Jersey's ___ Hall University
60 Novel ending?
61 1961 "spacechimp"
62 Wraps (up)
63 Accordion part

DOWN

1 Solver's online recourse
2 Allied (with)
3 Enjoyed doing
4 Title locale in a Cheech Marin flick
5 Actor Billy of "Titanic"
6 "What ___ boy am I!"
7 Adorned, in the kitchen
8 Super Bowl XXI M.V.P., first to say "I'm going to Disney World!"
9 What demonstrators demonstrate
10 Auto shop's offering
11 Longtime Cowboys coach Tom
12 Sort
15 Senate tally
21 Midback muscle, briefly
22 Villain
26 Suffix with Meso- or Paleo-
30 Ewe said it
31 Mann's "Der ___ in Venedig"
32 Singer DiFranco
33 Mosque V.I.P.
35 Things people are trained in?
36 Van Susteren of Fox News
37 Begin
38 Put up
39 Approached zero
42 Burial place of King Arthur
43 Ravel work
45 Unfriendly
46 Repertoire component
48 Senate tally
49 N.H.L. Eastern Conf. team
50 What a traveling salesman travels
51 Establish, as a chair
54 Department store section
55 Opposite of post-

by Henry Hook

66

ACROSS

1 Meat featured in a Monty Python musical title
5 Alternatives to PCs
9 Popeye's creator E. C. ___
14 "Look what I did!"
15 "There oughta be ___ !"
16 Singer Cara
17 Difficult burden
18 Many a stadium cover
19 Exxon competitor
20 Tourism bureau's offering
23 The matador's opponent
24 Totally cool, in '90s slang
25 Photo ___ (White House events)
28 It's swung at Wimbledon
32 J.F.K.'s successor
35 Ooze
36 1983 Barbra Streisand title role
37 Notes in a poker pot
39 It makes bread rise
42 Old-time wisdom
43 Kind of patch for a rabbit
45 Ark builder
47 Try to win, in romance
48 Pesky wasp
52 Communication means for the deaf: Abbr.
53 Cry when a light bulb goes on
54 Clears an Etch A Sketch, e.g.
58 It helps determine how much tax you owe the I.R.S.
62 Team leader
64 Venus de ___
65 Actress Spelling
66 Airs, in Latin
67 Suffix with switch
68 "The devil ___ the details"
69 King with a golden touch
70 Amount owed
71 Guitarist Atkins

DOWN

1 Vermont ski town
2 Group of experts
3 Like blue movies
4 Yale's bulldog, e.g.
5 Small amount of cash saved for an emergency
6 ___ vera
7 Pitch tents for the night
8 Says on a stack of Bibles
9 Time off from work with pay
10 Cleveland's lake
11 Become acquainted with
12 Lee who directed "Crouching Tiger, Hidden Dragon"
13 ___ Speedwagon
21 Miners' finds
22 Mercury or Saturn, but not Venus
26 Oil industry prefix
27 Canonized fifth-century pope
29 Born: Fr.
30 Classic toothpaste brand
31 Animation frame
32 Muammar el-Quaddafi's land
33 Makes yawn
34 Noted performing arts school
38 "My gal" of song
40 Party to the left of Dem.
41 Become established
44 Targets of Raid
46 Queen on Mount Olympus
49 A question of identity
50 Blocked, as radio broadcasts
51 Bit of strategy
55 Smidgen
56 Like "The Twilight Zone" music
57 Tour of duty
59 Univ. sports org.
60 Country whose name is an anagram of 10-Down
61 Unidentifiable mass
62 Film device, for short
63 Yves's yes

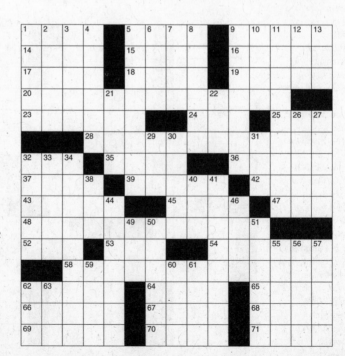

by Stella Daily and Bruce Venzke

ACROSS

1 Mag. sales info
5 Cat calls
10 Dutch cheese
14 Baseball's Matty or Felipe
15 First string
16 Danish-based toy company
17 Special Operations group
19 And
20 Makings of a hero, perhaps
21 Food giant that owns Ball Park Franks and Hillshire Farm
23 Domain
26 Tabula ___
27 Part of M.O.
30 Way back when
32 Welsh breed
35 Universal donor blood type, for short
36 Not susceptible
38 German article
39 Kilmer of film
40 Dr. ___ formerly of Death Row Records
41 Tiny amount
42 Coast Guard officer below lt.
43 "Richard ___"
44 Busybodies
46 "Hey there!"
47 War correspondent Pyle
49 Asian holiday
50 Nun, in Nanterre
51 N.F.L. periods: Abbr.
53 "The Wolf in Sheep's Clothing" author
55 Takes to the police station
58 New Jersey college until 1995
62 Biblical brother
63 Highly pleasing
66 Impart
67 Brooke's longtime rival on "All My Children"
68 "Rule, Britannia" composer
69 "Beetle Bailey" dog
70 Capital suggested by the circled letters and by the starts of 17- and 63-Across and 11- and 29-Down
71 Fails to keep

DOWN

1 Scoundrels
2 Intestinal parts
3 Sushi bar offering
4 Dance
5 Capo's organization
6 Ike's W.W. II arena
7 Done, to Donne
8 1954 war comedy "Francis Joins the ___"
9 Dirty political tactic
10 Rio Grande city
11 TV angel portrayer
12 Fit of shivering
13 Jazzman Allison
18 University town near Des Moines
22 Ran
24 "Alas, poor Yorick!," e.g.
25 RKO competitor
27 Picture
28 Studio sign
29 Overdue
31 Beat in a Nathan's hot dog contest, e.g.
33 Supersharp knife
34 Violin or cello: Abbr.
36 Fury
37 "Illmatic" rapper
40 Batik artists, e.g.
45 1773 jetsam in Boston Harbor
46 Britney Spears for one
48 "That's enough, I guess . . ."
50 Year before jr.
52 Allied
54 Cuban export
55 Heavenly circle
56 Help in mischief
57 Stout's Wolfe
59 Bushy do
60 Fontanne's stage partner
61 Publican's stock
64 Tyler of "Stealing Beauty"
65 Swelling reducer

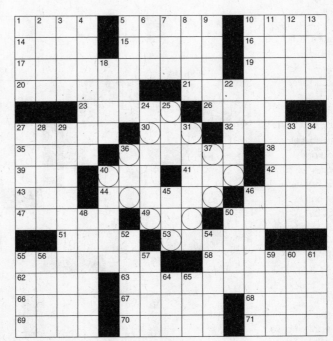

by Gary J. Whitehead

68

ACROSS

1 Course of action
5 Big jerk
10 Author O'Flaherty
14 Jai ___
15 White house
16 Suffix with govern
17 Musial's 6 and Gibson's 45?
20 Continuously
21 Grabs some shut-eye
22 Bitter drug
26 "Of course!"
27 Pregame practice in Cincinnati?
31 Sting operation
35 Dockworkers' org.
36 Beach washer
37 Go too far onstage
38 Leading the league
41 W.C.
42 Ledger entry
43 Coffeehouse order
44 Land O Lakes product
46 Air Force hero
47 Earl in the court of Elizabeth I
48 AT&T Park standout?
51 Music booster
53 Adak native
54 With "El," British victory site of 1942
58 Wild
62 Prospects for a New York pennant?
66 Operatic prince
67 Perrier alternative
68 Part of N.B.
69 Puts on
70 Query before a big event
71 Revue segment

DOWN

1 Snack in a shell
2 One of TV's "Two and a Half Men"
3 Give a hoot
4 Snatch
5 Sloth, for one
6 Eagle shooters' grp.
7 Every last bit
8 End of some company names
9 Pitcher's place
10 Inspiration for "Rent"
11 Don Juan's mother
12 Plot component
13 Post meal
18 Not playing
19 Hunted rodents
23 Go (for)
24 Closing passage
25 City in central Missouri
27 Long arm?
28 Inventor Howe
29 Indoor game much seen on English TV
30 Let slip
32 Go ___ for (defend)
33 Erie Canal city
34 Man of Principle?
39 Clambake fare
40 Adjective for a 1-Down
45 I might signify this
49 Clump of grass
50 Rathskeller decorations
52 Highland musician
54 In the center of
55 Block brand
56 Loads
57 Actress Campbell
59 Corner piece
60 Objecting to
61 Exam for a would-be atty.
63 Org. in "The Bourne Identity"
64 Tiny amount
65 To some extent

by Richard Silvestri

ACROSS

1 Exiled Ugandan Idi __
5 Home of the N.F.L.'s Buccaneers
10 Nile reptiles
14 "This __ be!"
15 Criminal's "a k a" name
16 Post-Christmas store event
17 Anglican body
19 "Wheel of Fortune" action
20 Former Roxy Music member Brian
21 Point a gun
22 Hornswoggled
23 Discover
25 Oration
28 Question when you can't tell two things apart
32 Number of Little Pigs
35 Egg layers
36 Kanga's kid in "Winnie-the-Pooh"
37 Shot in the arm
38 Duracell size
39 Like a score of 10 of a possible 10
41 Attys.' org.
42 Baseball glove
43 Not just mean
44 Jewish high holy day
48 Top secret?
49 The "I" of Canada's P.E.I.
53 Shady spot
55 Excellent service?
56 Whisper sweet nothings
57 Profound
58 Youth groups . . . with a hint to 17-, 28- and 44-Across
62 Autobahn auto
63 Chili con __

64 Suit to __
65 Seat for two or more
66 Has a bawl
67 Salon applications

DOWN

1 Needed a chiropractor, say
2 The Pine Tree State
3 Gold brick
4 To the __ degree
5 South Seas getaway
6 Homecoming attendee, for short
7 Old space station
8 __-10 Conference
9 Louisville Slugger wood
10 Per se
11 September birthstones
12 Ballet bend
13 E-mail command
18 Sign of prestige
22 Morning moisture
24 Flock females
25 Put away, as a sword
26 Something beaten at a party in Mexico
27 Letter before tee
29 __ longue
30 Jacket
31 Fit to be a saint
32 Skiers' lift
33 Tramp
34 Entree carved by a chef
39 "I'll be right there!"
40 Roald who wrote "James and the Giant Peach"
42 Treasure seeker's aid

45 Fanfare
46 "Ben-__"
47 Specialized markets
50 Less than 90 degrees
51 Prestigious prize awarded every December
52 Prescribed amounts
53 Commotions
54 Seized vehicle
55 "Rule, Britannia" composer
58 Agcy. that can fine TV stations
59 Crew's control?
60 Geller with a psychic act
61 Fall behind

by Randall J. Hartman

ACROSS

1 Perfect
6 Farm sound
9 Highly excited
13 Wispy clouds
14 Ash containers
16 Let go
17 Singers Clint + Patti
19 Couple in the news
20 Ache reliever
21 They may be sown
23 Fr. holy woman
24 It's jumped in a high jump
26 As high as you can possibly go
29 Pulitzer-winning biographer Leon
32 Singers Tom + Johnny
35 Where Kofi Annan earned his master's deg.
37 Says lovingly
38 Copacabana Beach locale
39 Classic film company . . . or a description of 17-, 32-, 46- and 65-Across?
43 Pharmaceutical watchdog grp.
44 Show subtitled "The American Tribal Love-Rock Musical"
45 "___ my shorts!": Bart Simpson
46 Singers Neil + Courtney
49 D.E.A. agent
52 "___ Deep" (1999 Omar Epps film)
53 Suffix with Caesar
55 Yale student
57 Midwestern tribe
60 Perched
63 Like Yul Brynner, famously
65 Singers James + Sly
67 Blue, in Bogotá
68 ___ Lee cakes

69 Poet Federico García ___
70 Prominent part of a Groucho disguise
71 "Wailing" instrument
72 Vows

DOWN

1 Cold war weaponry
2 Widen, as a pupil
3 Got rid of marks
4 Paths of pop-ups
5 Simile part
6 Accused's bad break
7 Uris hero
8 "Farm" dwellers
9 Vinegary
10 1960s sitcom with the catchphrase "Sorry about that, Chief"
11 Uplifting poem

12 Cameo, e.g.
15 Any ship
18 40-Down, e.g.
22 Heavenly
25 Cut again, as a turkey
27 Mother goddess in Egyptian mythology
28 Howe'er
30 British record label
31 John of "3rd Rock From the Sun"
33 Rocky hill
34 Bag with handles
36 Bluish hue
39 Tempura ___ (Japanese dish)
40 Vessel in "Twenty Thousand Leagues Under the Sea"
41 God, to Galileo
42 Where to board a train: Abbr.

43 Post-it note abbr.
47 Brain, slangily
48 Q-Tip target
50 "So's your old man!," e.g.
51 Grip tightly
54 Sine qua ___
56 "An invasion of armies can be resisted; an invasion of ___ cannot be resisted": Hugo
58 They may be crunched
59 Lima ladies: Abbr.
61 Norway's capital
62 Ancient Greek walkway
63 No-smoking ordinance, e.g.
64 ___ dye
66 ". . . ___ mouse?"

by Caleb Madison

ACROSS

1 Send roses, perhaps
4 Polo name
9 Pooh-pooh
14 "Atonement" author McEwan
15 Harvest bundle
16 Physics Nobelist Wolfgang
17 Singles bar habitué?
20 Twin in Genesis
21 Geog. feature
22 Intimate wear, informally
23 The Reds, on a scoreboard
25 H
27 Lie down on the job?
28 Do some barhopping?
33 "Rockaria!" grp.
34 Bogart role
35 Daft
39 Stooped shoulders, e.g.
41 Quick peek
43 Unagi or tekka maki
44 Ryan with 5,714 strikeouts
46 Eerie ability
47 Dirndls?
50 "Not if ___ help it!"
53 Santa ___ winds
54 Internists' grp.
55 Lye, e.g.
57 Pugilists' org.
60 In the matter of
63 "Wild and crazy guy" on the old "S.N.L."?
66 Put up with
67 Tear-out from a Playboy magazine
68 Rail-splitter's tool
69 Pick up on
70 Flabbergast
71 Football linemen, for short, caught in 17-, 28-, 47- and 63-Across?

DOWN

1 The "Judy" of Punch and Judy
2 Dinghy movers
3 This answer intersects it
4 East Lansing sch.
5 Call for attention
6 Monopoly expense
7 Certain marble
8 Not working
9 Washer or dryer action
10 Hold'em venue
11 Navel designation
12 Takes off
13 "For starters . . ."
18 Cease
19 Island shindig
24 Vicks brand
26 Two-position switch
28 Fires (up)
29 Baseball's Felipe or Moises
30 Gold: Prefix
31 Tended to by the butler, say
32 "A Life for the Tsar" composer
36 Callas or Sills
37 Alternative to "Hey!"
38 Informal assents
40 Death personified, in ancient Greece
42 Scale syllables
45 For the heck of it
48 Nuisance
49 Non-PC purchase
50 Feet in a meter
51 St. ___ of Assisi
52 Goodyear's home
56 Take a shine to
58 Eric of "Munich"
59 Santa ___, University of California city
61 ___ message
62 Sources of nickel, e.g.
64 Tax season V.I.P.
65 Zoo attraction

by Doug Peterson

ACROSS

1 The pyramids, for pharaohs
6 "Hey . . . over here!"
10 PBS newsman Lehrer
13 "The Cat and the Curmudgeon" author Cleveland ___
14 Inventor Elias
15 Absolutely the best
16 Place not generating rent
19 Feeling tied up, as a stomach
20 Rock band follower
21 "The first ___, the angel did say . . ."
23 Worked at, as a trade
24 Guarantees that mean nothing
30 Point again, as a gun
31 Crimped, as hair
32 Hit CBS drama with two spinoffs
35 Formal entrance
36 Euphoric
38 Pretend to be, as at a Halloween party
39 Without a prescription: Abbr.
40 Pal for Spot or Rover
41 Increase
42 Win that brings little actual gain
46 Avis competitor
48 Post-it, e.g.
49 Brandy cocktail
52 Warms up again
57 Contents of guns used in training exercises
59 Offerings to the poor
60 Dust Bowl migrant

61 New York footballer
62 Bad: Prefix
63 Baby boomers' kids, informally
64 Groups of buffalo

DOWN

1 Rikki-Tikki-___
2 Neighbor of Yemen
3 Make fun of
4 Kellogg's Raisin ___
5 Roget's listing
6 "Star Trek" weapon
7 Soak (up)
8 Booty
9 Ariz., e.g., before 1912
10 Portrayer of Frank Sinatra on "Saturday Night Live"

11 Concave belly button
12 Rationed (out)
15 Stubborn as ___
17 Feature of many a sports car
18 ___-turvy
22 Scuttlebutt
24 Therefore
25 Vegetarians avoid it
26 1998 Robin Williams title role
27 Common Father's Day gift
28 Off one's rocker
29 Climbing vine
33 Suffix with dino-
34 1960s Bill Cosby TV series
36 Baseball great Hodges
37 Words before "You may kiss the bride"
38 London hrs.

40 Group watched by Little Bo Peep
41 A pair of deuces beats it
43 Black cats and broken mirrors, by tradition
44 Whirlpool or tornado
45 Anatomical passage
46 Equally awful
47 Eli ___ and Company
50 Slip ___ (blunder)
51 Clean up leaves, e.g.
53 Actress McClurg
54 Food thickener
55 Care for, with "to"
56 Fleet that was permanently retired in 2003
58 ___ Tin Tin

by Mike Nothnagel

ACROSS

1 Break ground, in a way
5 Spill the beans
9 Come to an end
14 Boxcar hopper
15 After the buzzer
16 "The usual," e.g.
17 Active sort
18 Salem's state: Abbr.
19 Fare payer
20 Antlered salon employee?
23 Woodworker's groove
24 Actress Vardalos
25 Curly poker
28 Make darts, say
31 Lost bobcat?
34 Heebie-jeebies
36 Grab some Z's
37 Teed off
38 Train alternative
39 Vintner's valley
40 One with a pitch
43 Passé
45 Wildebeest who doesn't spare the rod?
47 Future alums: Abbr.
48 Approx. takeoff hr.
49 Here, in Haiti
50 Broadway musical with the song "Will I?"
52 Unwelcome porcine party attendee?
57 Crawfish's home
60 Tall story
61 Like some chatter
62 Continental divide?
63 Building extensions
64 Parks of Montgomery
65 Cops' rounds
66 European deer
67 Tiny amount

DOWN

1 Profs' degs.
2 Rioter's take
3 Toe the line
4 Word before class or war
5 Mrs. Bumstead
6 Slow movements, in music
7 "Up and ___!"
8 Showy blooms
9 Prom accessory
10 Toledo's lake
11 Throw in
12 Comprehend
13 Slip up
21 Big name in pet foods
22 Barnyard sound
25 Chatty avians
26 Even (with)
27 Nationals living abroad, informally
28 Genève's land
29 Wholly absorbed
30 Li'l fellow
32 Attacked by a jellyfish
33 Come to earth
35 Yemeni port
38 Something to slide on
41 Vail trails
42 Easily split mineral
43 Unity
44 Pulmonary organ
46 It's between the headlights
51 Rival of a 'Vette
52 Fur
53 Saintly sign
54 What wavy lines signify in the comics
55 As well
56 Gather in
57 Short do
58 1 or 11, in twenty-one
59 Roll call vote

by Billie Truitt

ACROSS

1 Irons or Woods
6 Iridescent gem
10 Classic clown
14 Old Big Apple restaurateur
15 Put blacktop on
16 Word repeated before "pants on fire"
17 Strap-on leg supports
19 Sister of Prince Charles
20 Reason for an R rating
21 Apple seeds' location
22 Film critic Gene
24 Without slack
25 Lady's partner
26 Cavalry cry
29 Experts with the ends of 17- and 55-Across and 10- and 24-Down
33 Eagle's nest
34 Cornmeal bread
35 Biblical flood survivor
36 Lame gait
37 Michelangelo masterpiece
38 Event proceeds
39 Fox's "American ___"
40 Away from the storm
41 Cancel, at Cape Canaveral
42 Rifle and revolver
44 Poisonous atmosphere
45 Part of a birthday celebration
46 Waste reservoir
47 Football refs
50 Mitchell who sang "Big Yellow Taxi"
51 "___ the season . . ."
54 "Peek-___, I see you!"
55 Mincemeat, e.g.
58 Gullet
59 Bones: Lat.
60 22-Across's longtime partner
61 Middle of many a steering wheel
62 Wed. follower
63 Things to salve

DOWN

1 Seeks info
2 Chaplin prop
3 "Jurassic Park" giant, informally
4 Poem often titled "To a . . ."
5 Chest protector
6 Some psychedelic designs
7 Show worry in the waiting room, maybe
8 "___ Maria"
9 Decreased
10 It sets things off
11 Sound piggish
12 Western writer Grey
13 Baseball's Hershiser
18 Rakish sort
23 Bank statement abbr.
24 Feat for Secretariat
25 Three wishes granter
26 Sacramento's state: Abbr.
27 Title heroine played by Shirley Temple in 1937
28 Knight's protection
29 Hawks' opposites
30 Goes up, up, up
31 Jazz great Art
32 "Come Back, Little ___"
34 ___ d'Or (Cannes award)
37 Appearing and disappearing feature on Jupiter
41 "Fresh as a daisy" and others
43 Org. that helps with tow service
44 Tax-exempt investment, for short
46 To date
47 2007 Masters champion Johnson
48 Longest Spanish river
49 Wild hog
50 Bach's "___, Joy of Man's Desiring"
51 Level
52 Legal memo starter
53 Some noncoms: Abbr.
56 Approximately: Suffix
57 Debt-incurring Wall St. deal

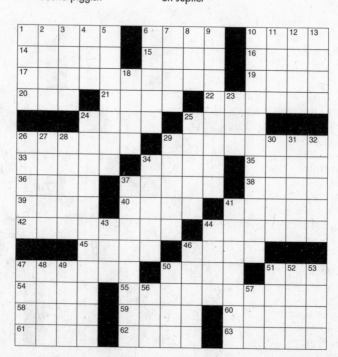

by Mark Sherwood

ACROSS

1 "Fall" guy
5 Three, it's said
10 Saks sack, say
14 Fries or slaw
15 Slot machine fruit
16 Enterprise alternative
17 E.S.L. class, perhaps?
20 Our base system
21 Word before fee or group
22 Main line
23 Harris's ___ Rabbit
24 It'll curl your hair
26 They're not original
29 Save for a rainy day
33 Diva's delivery
34 With 44-Down, "Wuthering Heights" actress
35 Title role for Will Smith
36 Seedy hangout across the Atlantic?
40 Web address ending
41 Down-and-out
42 Demon's doing
43 Bank receipts
45 Go to bat for
47 Makes verboten
48 Depend
49 Primp
52 Supreme Court count
53 Everyday article
56 Hip-hop critics?
60 Cookie with its name on it
61 Get off one's behind
62 Et ___
63 Hammer part
64 Meal with readings
65 1995 Physics Nobelist Martin L. ___

DOWN

1 Part of T.A.: Abbr.
2 Parcheesi pair
3 Mideast's Gulf of ___
4 Loo sign
5 Winds up
6 Direct, as for info
7 Actor Epps
8 Took all the marbles
9 Double-helix material
10 Puget Sound city
11 Frequent word from ham operators
12 TV control
13 "Cómo ___ usted?"
18 Lira's replacement
19 OPEC, e.g.
23 Kid you might feel like smacking
24 Kegger, e.g.
25 First name in scat
26 Did a 10K, e.g.
27 Eat away
28 Locker photo, maybe
29 Thrills
30 Give up
31 Chipmunk of pop music
32 Give up
34 Track team schedule
37 Out of one's mind
38 Ja's opposite
39 Go against
44 See 34-Across
45 Less astute
46 Gen. Robt. ___
48 Shampoo bottle instruction
49 Telephone on a stage, e.g.
50 Pink inside
51 Blunted blade
52 Reason to be barred from a bar . . . or the theme of this puzzle
53 Start to communicate?
54 "Aquarius" musical
55 Disney's "___ and the Detectives"
57 Carrier to Bergen
58 Opposite of post-
59 Bill (Bojangles) Robinson's forte

by Adam G. Perl

The New York Times

SMART PUZZLES
PRESENTED WITH STYLE

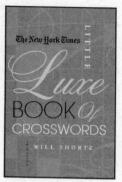

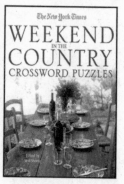

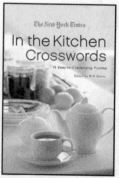

1

```
APPTS  NINE  ESTS
ASOUL  ENOS  NCAA
BYEBYELOVE  ORGY
ACT  ALI  BLESS
 HIYOSILVERAWAY
 ECARTE ELO ULE
 SAXE  ORB  APES
  ILLBEBACK
MBAS  AER  HIPS
ELL  INE  ARETOO
SOLONGFAREWELL
HAHAS  BAN  AVG
UTES  YOUREFIRED
GERI  ALTA  AKIRA
ADES  PEST  MESSY
```

2

```
SALAD  ESQ  POSTS
ADELE  PEU  IVORY
SHELF  AMI  NEXUS
HORSERUSTLER
ACS  CUL  IAN  ERE
 STEELTRUSSES
ABBA  STA  STATES
PLANB  STL  STEVE
AORTAS  EOS  ERES
ROBERTSRULES
TDS  FAT  GON  GOA
 MIXEDRESULTS
DORAG  AAA  UNITS
ECASH  MTN  EDDIE
NTEST  YET  DOEST
```

3

```
DAUNT  OCTAD  BOP
ASTOR  ROYCE  ANA
HEAVIESTPUMPKIN
LAH  ENOTE  ERECT
 ASANA  TRADES
EBERT  REID
LONGESTMUSTACHE
ANG  AEONS  HIE
LARGESTMEATBALL
 ASHE  ROILS
OMERTA  NOLAN
CARTE  MOLES  ROD
HIGHESTHIGHDIVE
ENO  MAGOO  EXCEL
RET  SLEWS  DIANE
```

4

```
CALF  BRUIN  ACCT
OLEO  REPRO  GORE
TFORMATION  ILET
SASSY  INN  ALLAH
 ARON  OPIATE
PICKOFTHELITTER
TORENT  AYEAYE
ANI  LYE  RAW
 MAGPIE  RAVAGE
CHERRIESJUBILEE
LOSTIT  ETON
ELCID  PAR  VENTI
ADES  BUCKROGERS
TENT  OLLIE  ARIA
SMEE  BLUNT  ROXY
```

5

```
TOSS  ABEAM  SETS
SHOO  ROSSI  AGHA
AIRY  GNATS  TRIG
ROTARYDIAL  YEGG
 ILS  EARTHY
DEMOTE  MAAM
OCALA  GOLDCOAST
FORD  SOAPS  BLAH
FLESHTONE  BIOME
 BUDS  SATEEN
SPOTON  SAL
NUKE  TURTLEDOVE
IRAN  MEARA  USED
PIPE  ALTAR  SLID
EMIT  NEEDY  TONY
```

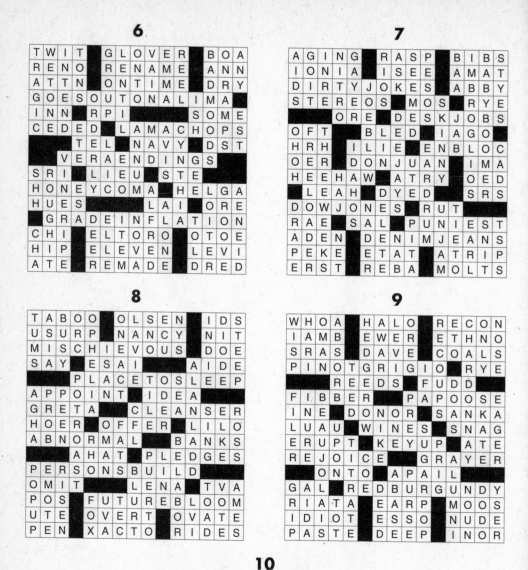

6

```
T W I T   G L O V E R   B O A
R E N O   R E N A M E   A N N
A T T N   O N T I M E   D R Y
G O E S O U T O N A L I M A
I N N   R P I       S O M E
C E D E D   L A M A C H O P S
      T E L   N A V Y   D S T
    V E R A E N D I N G S
S R I   L I E U   S T E
H O N E Y C O M A   H E L G A
H U E S       L A I   O R E
  G R A D E I N F L A T I O N
C H I   E L T O R O   O T O E
H I P   E L E V E N   L E V I
A T E   R E M A D E   D R E D
```

7

```
A G I N G   R A S P   B I B S
I O N I A   I S E E   A M A T
D I R T Y J O K E S   A B B Y
S T E R E O S   M O S   R Y E
      O R E   D E S K J O B S
O F T   B L E D   I A G O
H R H   I L I E   E N B L O C
O E R   D O N J U A N   I M A
H E E H A W   A T R Y   O E D
  L E A H   D Y E D   S R S
D O W J O N E S   R U T
R A E   S A L   P U N I E S T
A D E N   D E N I M J E A N S
P E K E   E T A T   A T R I P
E R S T   R E B A   M O L T S
```

8

```
T A B O O   O L S E N   I D S
U S U R P   N A N C Y   N I T
M I S C H I E V O U S   D O E
S A Y   E S A I     A I D E
  P L A C E T O S L E E P
A P P O I N T   I D E A
G R E T A   C L E A N S E R
H O E R   O F F E R   L I L O
A B N O R M A L   B A N K S
  A H A T   P L E D G E S
P E R S O N S B U I L D
O M I T   L E N A   T V A
P O S   F U T U R E B L O O M
U T E   O V E R T   O V A T E
P E N   X A C T O   R I D E S
```

9

```
W H O A   H A L O   R E C O N
I A M B   E W E R   E T H N O
S R A S   D A V E   C O A L S
P I N O T G R I G I O   R Y E
      R E E D S   F U D D
F I B B E R   P A P O O S E
I N E   D O N O R   S A N K A
L U A U   W I N E S   S N A G
E R U P T   K E Y U P   A T E
R E J O I C E   G R A Y E R
  O N T O   A P A I L
G A L   R E D B U R G U N D Y
R I A T A   E A R P   M O O S
I D I O T   E S S O   N U D E
P A S T E   D E E P   I N O R
```

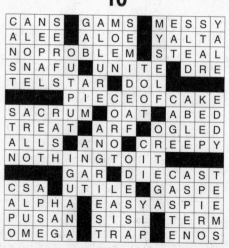

10

```
C A N S   G A M S   M E S S Y
A L E E   A L O E   Y A L T A
N O P R O B L E M   S T E A L
S N A F U   U N I T E   D R E
T E L S T A R   D O L
    P I E C E O F C A K E
S A C R U M   O A T   A B E D
T R E A T   A R F   O G L E D
A L L S   A N O   C R E E P Y
N O T H I N G T O I T
    G A R   D I E C A S T
C S A   U T I L E   G A S P E
A L P H A   E A S Y A S P I E
P U S A N   S I S I   T E R M
O M E G A   T R A P   E N O S
```

11

```
BANG  INFER  BLUR
AGUE  MILLE  LORE
LEMONPLUMORANGE
DEBRA    SPONGED
   GRIPE  ELK
SEVENSEVENLEMON
CRO  IMPEL  TALE
RIT ASL IDS ODE
UKES  UPSET RID
BARPLUMCHERRIES
  ION  SAMOA
SPECIES   PRADO
SEVENSEVENSEVEN
TSAR  CLARA  FILE
SONY  OFTEN  YVES
```

12

```
SHAH  PSST  SCENE
TONO  OTIS  ARGON
AUTO  LENA  LOGIC
TRIPLEWORDSCORE
  FLUB   YAK
AERATE  SHE  PUFF
STE  HASTA  DONOR
THECONSERVATORY
RAZOR  TAKEN  RTE
ONER  ASK  SISTER
   NAY   TECH
READINGRAILROAD
EPSOM  RUNG  IDLE
BEIGE  ALEE  BOOM
SENSE  MEWS  EXES
```

13

```
CPAS  ONSET  ASIS
HERE  PEKOE  GENA
ASCERTAINS  ACTV
DOSSIER  TIPTOE
  OLDSAW  TEA
ONCUE  NAPA  RAH
MEAT  SEAGAL  IRA
APR  SURGERY  AIR
HAT  HEARSE  GNAT
ALE  ESTA  HESSE
  SIR  OMELET
CHISEL  MARIMBA
HEAL  ISAACSTERN
ANNE  MOVIE  OMIT
PSST  OPALS  NOTE
```

14

```
LEAVE  GETS  STOW
ALCOA  EXIT  TORI
GIRLS  LEGO  OUTS
  OVERSCHLEPPED
INSOLE  TED  EGO
CAT  SAGAS  IBEAM
EPIC  GYM  ETO
  SCHNAPPSSHOTS
  ION  LIP  SHAW
AMINO  BERRA  IRA
TON  STE  IRANIS
HOCKEYSCHTICK
ORAL  SIRE  SCENT
MESA  ODOR  ERROR
EDEN  NEWS  NASTY
```

15

```
AREA  TAMP  SPEAK
DADS  EVIL  EERIE
HIGHGRADE  LAIRD
ONAPAR  DATELESS
CYRIL  OLDEN
  TORRE  NAMELY
ALA  RELOAD  TRIO
CENTEROFGRAVITY
ROTO  ENTAIL  NEO
ENIGMA  HILTS
  ADMEN  AMIRS
CLEANSER  LIONEL
HABIT  LOWERCASE
ATOLL  BAAS  KNEE
TENSE  ADDS  SEEP
```

16

```
H A V O C   G I D E   P R E Z
A R E N A   A D E N   R O S E
N E G E V   N E A T   O U T A
G S A   E L D E R H O S T E L
    G R O H   R A I S E S
L O G A N A I R P O R T
E V I L S   E O N S   B I B
D I L L   C O N D E   N A N O
A D D   S A N E   B E R R Y
    S T R A W C O L O R E D
O B R I E N   L I O N
B L U E P E N C I L S   D U E
E I N S   G O O N   S O R R Y
S N I T   I S A K   O S A G E
E D N A   E E L S   M E T E R
```

17

```
C C S   A C L U   A G A S S I
L O U   M O O T   S O B E I T
A M P   A N N A   H O O P L A
W E E K N I G H T   D R I L L
    R E A C H   E C S T A S Y
A B B Y     A S L O P E
R E O   T A N K   R O D N E Y
C A W   E N D U S E R   E R A
S U L T A N   N E S T   W O W
    A L A S K A   A S S N
C A N C E L S   S C A M P
E V I T A   W O O D S C R E W
N A T I V E   S N I T   I K E
T I T L E D   L A I R   N E E
S L I E S T   O L I O   T S P
```

18

```
R S V P S   L A T E R   L B J
O P E R A   A R O S E   E R A
B A N A N A S E A T S   M A D
E T A L   P T A S   A N O D E
    S L I C E S   T A L O N
    N O R T H   S E A L E D
E L D E R   R O U T   H A R E
Y E A   N E A T N I K   W I N
E A T S   A W E D   E A S E S
D R E A D S   L E N D L
    B R U T E   R O S T E R
G R O A N   B E G S   O L E O
R I O   C H E R R Y B O M B S
I N K   A O R T A   O N E A L
M D S   N O T E D   L A R G O
```

19

```
D E M I   D E A R   F I D E S
I V A N   A B B E   I D I O T
C E R F   V O I D   R E S E E
E N D U R I N G F A M E
    T I L E D   A I N U   M I R
    L A S T I N G P E A C E
A M A   P O O L   A R I D
D E M E S N E   A W F U L L Y
E L A N   O A R S   A Y E
A B I D I N G F A I T H
L A N   N E U F   N O O S E
    S T A Y I N G P O W E R
S P I T E   A C E D   T O R O
K A R E N   N E A R   E R I C
A D E P T   A R T Y   R E E K
```

20

```
R O C K Y   D R O P   M E L T
I N A N E   R A V E   A P E R
B E S O T   A G E E   R O V E
    S T I C K E R P R I C E S
C H E   O E D   H A S H E S
H A T R E D   F O E
A R T I N   F O O L   I D E A
F E E S C H A R G E D B Y A N
E S S E   A I R Y   D I N G O
    E R R   M E D A L S
S E N E C A   S K I   S E E
A C U P U N C T U R I S T
W O R E   G O A D   T A I L S
E L S E   U P T O   C R E E L
D I E S   E Y E S   H A S T Y
```

21

A	S	H	E		S	C	A	L	D		W	H	A	M
S	T	O	P		H	U	M	O	R		H	O	P	I
S	O	S	O		I	R	O	N	Y		O	Y	E	Z
A	L	E	X	A	N	D	R	E	D	U	M	A	S	
M	E	R	Y	L				R	E	P				
			D	A	T	A		N	O	N	C	O	M	
A	L	L	F	O	R	O	N	E		N	E	U	R	O
L	A	I	R		T	R	E	V	I		A	B	E	L
A	Z	T	E	C		O	N	E	F	O	R	A	L	L
S	E	E	T	H	E		T	S	A	R				
			I	D	A				E	S	S	A	Y	
	T	H	A	T	I	S	O	U	R	M	O	T	T	O
S	H	A	Q		S	O	U	S	A		F	O	O	D
P	E	R	U		O	N	S	E	T		A	N	N	E
Y	O	D	A		N	E	E	D	S		R	E	E	L

22

L	O	K	I		L	E	A	R	N		G	A	G	A
E	R	I	N		E	M	C	E	E		A	R	E	S
W	E	N	D		G	O	O	S	E	F	L	E	S	H
D	O	G	I	E		R	E	D	O		E	T	E	
	C	A	R	D	I	N	A	L	R	U	L	E	S	
L	E	O		R	O	B		T	E	E	N			
O	R	B		O	D	I	E			U	H	O	H	
P	A	R	T	R	I	D	G	E	F	A	M	I	L	Y
E	S	A	U			G	L	O	M		N	E	D	
		B	A	H	T		A	R	E		D	O	E	
	C	A	N	A	R	Y	I	S	L	A	N	D	S	
A	L	I		L	E	N	T			D	R	I	P	S
P	I	G	E	O	N	H	O	L	E		A	G	R	A
E	C	H	O		A	A	R	O	N		W	H	E	N
S	E	T	S		S	T	E	A	D		S	T	Y	E

23

A	K	R	O	N		M	E	S	H		G	L	O	P
D	R	A	C	O		A	L	P	O		H	I	V	E
M	O	N	S	T	E	R	H	I	T		O	M	A	R
I	N	K		R	E	S	I	N		P	S	A	L	M
T	A	S	S	E	L		S	L	O	T				
		K	A	Y	A	K		U	N	W	I	S	E	
L	A	B	E	L		B	A	C	K	D	R	O	P	S
O	P	E	L		M	E	L	E	E		I	N	I	T
F	I	R	E	W	A	T	E	R		S	T	A	T	E
T	A	M	T	A	M		S	T	A	L	E			
		O	R	A	L		N	A	R	R	O	W		
B	R	I	N	E		O	I	N	K	S		A	B	A
R	O	C	K		W	I	T	C	H	H	A	Z	E	L
A	L	O	E		A	R	E	A		E	R	O	S	E
D	E	N	Y		H	E	R	R		D	A	R	E	S

24

C	A	L	F		A	M	M	O		S	T	E	N	O
A	S	I	A		L	I	O	N		T	E	N	O	R
T	H	E	D	A	B	A	R	A		O	X	I	D	E
S	E	T		T	E	T	E		G	L	A	D	E	S
	S	O	P	H	I	A	L	O	R	E	N			
		L	E	T		M	A	N		G	A	M		
W	O	M	A	N		L	E	A	N		C	A	M	E
E	L	I	Z	A	B	E	T	H	T	A	Y	L	O	R
B	E	T	A		R	O	S	A		S	N	A	K	E
S	O	T		P	A	X		A	L	D				
	V	I	V	I	E	N	L	E	I	G	H			
C	A	L	I	C	O		N	I	L	E		E	O	S
A	B	A	C	K		C	L	E	O	P	A	T	R	A
P	E	N	A	L		R	A	C	Y		H	U	N	K
S	T	A	R	E		T	I	E	S		A	P	S	E

25

R	E	H	A	B		A	W	A	R	D		B	I	D
A	R	E	N	A		P	O	L	A	R		I	S	O
P	A	R	T	Y	P	O	O	P	E	R		G	E	E
T	S	E		W	E	L	L	S		U	N	S	E	R
		F	A	L	L			A	T	O	P			
P	L	A	T	F	O	R	M	S	H	O	E	S		
B	R	O	N	C		A	R	I		K	N	O	T	
L	I	V		H	I	N	T	S	A	T		D	U	O
T	M	E	N		R	O	T		E	M	E	R	Y	
	P	R	I	M	A	R	Y	C	O	L	O	R	S	
		S	C	A	N		A	B	L	E				
A	L	L	E	N		A	U	D	I	T		T	O	E
V	I	A		T	I	C	K	E	T	A	G	E	N	T
I	A	N		E	G	R	E	T		L	E	N	T	O
D	R	E		L	O	E	S	S		E	L	T	O	N

26

```
A T L   H A S O N   R I C K S
T E A   O S T E O   E T A I L
D E T   W H E N P I G S F L Y
A T O M S     E N A M E L
W H Y Y O U L I T T L E
N E A L   N U N S     T E D
    O D I S T   S E A W A Y
W H E R E T H E B O Y S A R E
R U N D R Y   G L U E S
Y E S     I R E S   E M I T
  W H A T A W A Y T O G O
  I D I O T S     O S H E A
W H O L O V E S Y O U   A T T
O O Z E D   L A U E R   V I E
O P E D S   F O L D S   E T E
```

27

```
A P E R   T I E D   S H E L F
R E G U L A R L Y   P A T I O
T W O B U C K L E M Y S H O E
E S S E N   E S S O   T A N S
      G A D     E G A N
  E S T E R   R A T A   F O B
A C N E   C H E R   Z O R B A
F O U R S H U T T H E D O O R
A L F I E   G A Y E   I M E T
R E F   A D O G   R E N E S
    B A L I     C O M
A P O P   S O S O   P H A S E
S I X P I C K U P S T I C K S
K E E L S   A M A R Y L L I S
A S S E T   Y O Y O   L U T E
```

28

```
S T E A L   S O A P   S P R Y
G H A N A   A B L E   Q U A D
T A C K S   T E S T   U R I S
  W H A T D O Y O U C A L L
      W I N S   L B S
A L A N I S     A S H O R T
L O B E S   I M I N   R O O
P S Y C H I C O N T H E L A M
H E S   L E E K   A R O S E
A S M A L L     E V E N T S
    N O H   P I L E
  M E D I U M A T L A R G E
M A S H   M I S S   C A I N E
O R S O   O N T O   O R B I T
M E O W   R E E K   W E E D S
```

29

```
S A F E   S W A T S   O W E D
I T L L   T H R O E   L I V E
A L U M   R E A D E   D R E W
M A T T H E W M O D I N E
E N T R A P     S E T T O
S T E E R   M A R K T W A I N
E A R E D   I S E E   S P A T
      G O S P E L S
M O S S   N E E D   H A D E S
L U K E P E R R Y   A M I S H
I R I N A     P R O N T O
  J O H N D I L L I N G E R
S P U R   E E R I E   G I L T
L I M A   L L A M A   S E L L
Y A P S   L I N E D   T R A Y
```

30

```
G U L P   S W A T H   M E T S
O P I E   C H I N A   A L O E
B O L T F R O M T H E B L U E
I N T E R I M     L E E R S
    R I P   F R A I L
E C H O   T A L O N   L A B S
T R A S H   R O D E O   D I P
H A V E A S C R E W L O O S E
E V E   G O T I N   E L B O W
R E N T   F I S T S   D E N S
    R E A C T   H E M
A F L A T     C O R O L L A
D E A D A S A D O O R N A I L
D A V E   A T A R I   E M M A
S T A R   Y E M E N   Y E A S
```

31

```
MONS _ GAOL _ SYNE
AMAH _ LENTO _ HOOD
LEGOMUTTON _ AGED
AGAWAM _ SEGOLILY
RATEDPG _ ORO _
_ DAYOJUDGMENT
ALBUM _ TANDY _ DEY
PERP _ WHIPS _ YEAR
EVA _ CHIME _ RANTO
RIGHTOCENTER _
_ INC _ SOLDIER
FAILSAFE _ DIANNE
ELAL _ RINGOTRUTH
EDGE _ ELVES _ MIRE
TOOL _ SLYE _ STEM
```

32

```
SEWN _ PROF _ PEDES
LUAU _ ROTE _ HROSS
ERIC _ AARE _ YOWLS
DOLLEYMADISON _
_ ESS _ MMI _ FTD
_ HIPTOBESQUARE
SRO _ OAR _ OUTLET
HEMAN _ TAB _ EELER
OCELOT _ GAT _ ESE
ROOFTOPGARDEN _
NNW _ ARR _ EON _
_ NEWYORKKNICKS
OBEAH _ WEEK _ GRAM
FARSI _ ANNI _ MIRE
ASSET _ ROSE _ ABLE
```

33

```
SALEM _ LISPS _ TOP
AMANA _ INERT _ UPI
GAYDIVORCEE _ BET
ETO _ TENETS _ RACY
TINEAR _ OOZE _
_ GINGERROGERS
LUNG _ EEL _ TOATEE
AHARD _ OCT _ TITAN
DODOES _ IRK _ NERD
SHALLWEDANCE _
_ LIEN _ ORDEAL
BANS _ ADESTE _ LIE
ARE _ FREDASTAIRE
SIX _ ABANG _ INTER
HAT _ MYRAS _ NEEDY
```

34

```
MELT _ FARE _ CIGAR
ASIA _ OFIT _ OCULI
LASTDITCH _ LETGO
TIPTOE _ EEL _ STET
_ LUGE _ LASHERS
INTEGRAL _ PEER _
MER _ HAGAR _ WEBER
ARES _ SEMIS _ TAPE
TONIC _ RECTO _ LED
_ CZAR _ SKIPOLES
SPHERES _ STEP _
COCA _ BEL _ CREATE
ADOBE _ TVCHANNEL
RIALS _ TORE _ ITEM
FATES _ OVID _ TESS
```

35

```
GEESE _ PAST _ TWOD
PRAWN _ EDIE _ ROBE
AIREDAZZLE _ ERIN
SENDER _ ETTAKETT
_ ERAT _ YER _
PECS _ GOA _ RAMADA
AGA _ FONDA _ MANET
PERSONNELFIZZLE
ASTON _ ELIAS _ IVS
STANDS _ ABC _ POET
_ LTS _ ITSA _
RIVIERAS _ UPNESS
EVEN _ ARMYMUZZLE
PAID _ IGOR _ RERUN
ONLY _ NEGS _ TRAMS
```

36

```
T H A T   G R I N S   E L S E
H E R A   E A S E D   S O M E
E L M S   T I S H A   T S A R
W E A K I N T H E K N E E S
A N D   T O T E M   O R T H O
Y E A R S     I A N   I U D
    E M T   H A D J   M P S
  E A S Y O N T H E E Y E S
P V C   T R I S   E W E
T I E   U N C     I N F O R
A L T A R   O U S T S   R N A
  D O W N A T T H E H E E L S
B O N A   R I T E S   C R I P
R E E K   K N E L T   R E N E
O R S E   S E R F S   U S E D
```

37

```
T H E M   S A S S   C D R O M
H O P E   E S T A   A R O M A
U N I T   T H A N   T A M E R
S E C R E T A G E N T M A N
    O N E R     O L A
M A J   D E P E C H E   A S H
E L I H U     A S I   A L T O
S E M I P R I V A T E R O O M
A R M S   U K E   A T O N E
S T Y   K N E S S E T   F E D
    S N O   I V E S
  L A C O N F I D E N T I A L
H A S A T   A G I N   U S N A
S T I N T   T O N S   F E N D
T E S T Y   E R G O   F E E S
```

38

```
A C R E   C R I E R   C A M P
R A I N   L O O S E   A R I A
O F F T H E O U T S   S A L T
M E T   A R T S   T R I B E S
A S S I S I   C A A N
    O N C O L O R J O K E S
P A I N T   H A S T A   I L E
A M P S   D E R M S   S N I T
L E S   F U N G I   S O D A S
O N O N E S R O C K E R
    A T T Y   O T T E R S
B A L S A M   O S S A   M A E
A D O S   O F F T H E M E N D
L E S E   P E A L E   U R G E
L E E R   S E N O R   D Y E R
```

39

```
F A L S E   A L O H A   S R S
E L E C T   P A T O N   T I N
I S A A C N E W T O N   E G O
N O R M   O R L O P   A V O W
    P A U S E   L I T E R S
B A A I N G   S T A M E N
L T D   D A I S Y   M A J O R
E M A N A T E   P R O M O T E
W O M E N   S N E E R   B O A
    A S T U T E   T A S S E L
C E N T E R   S W I L L
L A D Y   S A T A N   A M O S
A R E   W I L L I A M T E L L
M T V   A N D E S   C E L L O
S H E   Y E A S T   I D T A G
```

40

```
C E L E B   A D O     P A P A
A L E V E   J E W   M O N A D
S U G A R C A N E   U R G E D
E D U   L U X E   A S T R A L
R E P A I R   B I S C A Y N E
    S O S O   T I L L
C I T I Z E N K A N E   T A J
A D E S   S O L   A E R O
B O X   R A I S I N G C A I N
    A I N T   C A R E
H E R B C A E N   C O R A L S
A M U L E T   O A H U   B A T
N I N E R   N O V O C A I N E
G L O S S   A N O   H I N G E
S E N T   P E W   O R D E R
```

41

```
G R A S S   P L O   S M O K E
S I N A I   L A C   E I D E R
A D D L E   A T T E N D I N G
      M R S T H E P O I N T
S A T I R E   S T I R
E T H   A V E   S C I S S O R
A T E   E L M   T I L D E
M I S S I N F O R M A T I O N
A L I E N   P I E   E N D
N A S T I E R   P C B   S T E
        T A O S   C A P T O R
    M R B I R T H D A Y S
N E U R A L G I A   O A R E D
A R I E L   U R N   U L T R A
G E N T S   T E A   S M E A R
```

42

```
S P A R K Y   S E S   G A M
T I T H E D   C H A W   O R E
E A T E R S   H E R A   O T T
A N I O N   S A L L Y   D I E
D O C   E N T R   Y E A G E R
      B L U E L Y   R R R
I T S O   K I E V   S T I P E
S A C S   E N S O R   F E L L
H O H U M   E S N E   U F O S
    R N A   M C N E I L
G H O S T S   H E L M   P A S
R A E   L I N U S   S M A L L
A N D   E T A L   S U B T L E
D O E   S I T Z   P R A T E D
S I R   S N O   Y E S Y E S
```

43

```
O S H A   A B O M B   M A M A
A L E C   T I B E R   O M E N
R O A R   O P E R A   B O A T
  B R O W N E Y E D G I R L
    S H E D   S A L
H A S T A   S A M   S E L M A
A T T I C S   L O U   L A I
B L A C K E Y E D S U S A N S
L A B   X I V   E N A M E L
A S S E T   N E W   T R A D E
    Y A K   H A I G
  G R E E N E Y E D L A D Y
B O I L   O L A N D   S E E P
O N C E   W I N C E   S E A L
B E E T   N A K E D   O P R Y
```

44

```
A M P S   D U O S   S T A S H
M A I L   A N N E   C A R T E
E D D A   D I E M   O X B O W
B E G T H E Q U E S T I O N
A D I E U   U P S E T   R E D
S O N   M A E   T E Y   E A R
    D O S   E E K   B A G S
  B O R R O W T R O U B L E
D A V Y   C O S   U M S
E N E   S I R   S T P   S P A
F I R   T A S S O   E A T I T
  S T E A L T H I R D B A S E
A T I L T   O I L Y   O R C A
F E M M E   F R E E   V E E S
T R E S S   F E D S   E S S E
```

45

```
D O O R   P R I M   T A M P A
A L S O   L E N O   O N E A L
M A L T   A S T O   S T A I D
E V O C A T I O N   T I N G E
        L E S   T A S T E R
S C O P E   T H I R D
A L L I E S   E Q U A L I T Y
F A D E   M I D S T   A R O O
E M E R G I N G   H A Z A R D
        A R N E L   P E N T A
R E M A R K   O S O
A L A R M   E Q U I P P I N G
J E S S E   R U N T   A V O N
A N T O N   M A G I   R A G A
H A S N T   A D E N   K N O W
```

46

```
P A D S   P R I S M   W E D S
L I O N   H A R T E   I T A L
A R N O   O N E A T   S U M O
Z E N   O T I S R E D D I N G
A D A G I O     T O R O
    F O L S O M   R A M J E T
O P A L S   D E N I M   O R O
L O R D   S O N I C   S H A M
D O G   A U R A L   S E N S E
S H O G U N   T E S T E D
    O D D S     M U S E U M
P A T T I A U S T I N   N B A
A L U M   N E P A L   A V O N
L I R A   C R A T E   T E A S
L A N D   E S S E S   A R T E
```

47

```
L S A T   P I A F   E F L A T
A C T A   O L L A   Q U O T H
T A B C O L L A R   U N C L E
E L A I N E   N I P A T
L A T T I C E   N A B   A P E
Y R S   C A B C A L L O W A Y
    M E T R O   L E S A G E
S P A Y   O N A   L Y E S
C O H O S T   A N G L O
A R A B C O U N T R Y   F I R
R E B   H E N   S A R D I N E
    A U D I O   B I E R C E
A T A L L   C R A B C A K E S
R E L I T   E A V E   R I S E
B L I T Z   F L E D   E N T S
```

48

```
A D O S   E S P   U S A B L E
R U T H   A T E   S C R E E N
R O B I N S O N   S H I N E D
    N O T I N G   M D C C I
R B I   S E C   E R I   H H S
Y A S S E R   T H E D A
A L L C E N T U R Y T E A M
N E E R   A R I   O D A S
    S T A R T I N G L I N E U P
    M A I L S   O N S A L E
S S S   T O O   O C T   L S D
O P E R A   R I P K E N
C O G I T O   W I L L I A M S
K O U F A X   A N E   M A Y S
S L E E T Y   S E T   S H O T
```

49

```
T I L T   A L E S   A L O E S
A R I A   D O Z E   T A S T E
C O R N   V A I L   E N S U E
O N A G A I N O F F A G A I N
    O N C E     U S E
O F T   T E R M I T E   N A P
P A R I S   O R O   L O C A
E V E R Y N O W A N D T H E N
R O A R   O R E   E D I T S
A R T   S T A R T U P   T O Y
    D I E   O N O S
I N F I T S A N D S T A R T S
T A L E S   C O A T   R E A L
A M I G O   I N T O   A L P O
L E T O N   D E E P   N Y S E
```

50

```
E S P   J I G S   A N W A R
O L E G   A G R A   N O R M A
N A N A   G O O K   A T E A T
  W A L P U R G I S N A C H T
    L E A   T I N K L Y
S T G E O R G E S D A Y
P E R O N   H R O S S   M M E
E R I N   A R R   K I E V
W I N   C A N O E   T E N S E
    S O L A R N E W Y E A R
I S T H M I   D I E
P A N A M E R I C A N D A Y
A T O N E   A D A M   U L A N
S A T I N   J O K E   P I L E
S N E A D   A L E S   T E D
```

51

S	W	A	B		D	I	M	E	S		K	A	Y	E
O	H	N	O		E	V	E	N	T		A	W	A	Y
W	O	O	F		C	A	R	L	A		P	E	K	E
S	A	N	F	R	A	N	C	I	S	C	O			
		O	A	R			S	H	O	W	O	F	F	
A	R	C		F	L	O	U	T	E	D		R	E	L
B	O	Y	S	T	O	W	N		S	A	N	D	R	A
A	C	N	E		N	B	A			B	E	R	M	
S	K	I	E	R	S		A	D	A	M	S	R	I	B
E	N	C		E	T	A	G	E	R	E		S	S	E
D	E	S	K	S	E	T		M	A	C				
		S	P	E	N	C	E	R	T	R	A	C	Y	
J	O	L	T		P	O	O	L	E		O	U	Z	O
A	R	E	A		L	O	P	E	S		C	R	A	W
B	E	A	R		E	N	A	C	T		K	A	R	L

52

	S	T	U	D		Q	I	D		N	O	M	A	D
	W	O	R	E		U	N	A		O	P	I	N	E
F	O	O	L	F	A	I	N	T		B	I	L	G	E
A	R	K	S		E	R	I	E		O	U	T	E	R
R	E	N		F	R	E	E		A	D	M	I	R	E
G	O	O	G	O	O		P	R	Y		E	S	S	
O	F	T	W	O		P	U	R	I	S	T			
	F	E	E	L	L	I	K	E	A	F	O	O	L	
			N	I	E	C	E	S		E	R	V	I	N
M	I	T		N	I	K		G	E	N	E	V	A	
I	N	R	A	G	S		I	D	O	L		R	E	V
A	C	E	T	O		K	N	O	B		A	S	W	E
S	H	A	R	K		A	P	R	I	L	F	E	E	L
M	E	D	I	A		Y	U	M		I	T	L	L	
A	S	S	A	Y		O	T	S		T	A	L	L	

53

R	A	G	A		S	E	A	U		Q	T	R	S	
A	J	A	R		O	W	I	N	G		U	R	A	L
H	A	P	P	Y	B	I	R	T	H	D	A	Y	T	O
		S	I	E	V	E			A	V	A	S	T	
I	L	A		E	S	E		R	A	Z	E			
C	I	R	C	L	E	L	E	T	T	E	R	S	T	O
I	N	R	E	D		J	E	W	S		O	H	M	
N	E	I	L		A	N	E	S	T		C	R	E	E
G	U	V		E	X	E	C		K	N	E	L	L	
S	P	E	L	L	O	U	T	T	H	E	N	A	M	E
		A	I	N	T		H	A	Y		T	A	T	
D	A	R	T	H		R	E	B	U	S				
O	F	Y	O	U	R	R	E	C	I	P	I	E	N	T
C	R	A	Y		A	I	M	A	T		Z	E	E	S
K	O	N	A		F	A	I	R		E	L	B	E	

54

A	M	I	N		C	R	A	W		Z	A	P	P	A
S	A	N	E		A	N	N	A		A	D	O	R	N
F	I	R	S	T	L	A	D	Y		N	O	S	E	D
O	N	E	T	O			S	A	S	E		S	S	E
R	E	S		S	E	C	O	N	D	G	U	E	S	S
		E	D	S	E	L		S	I	R	S			
A	C	R	E		L	U	X		E	A	S	E	L	
C	O	V	E	R	S	E	V	E	R	Y	B	A	S	E
C	R	E	P	E		I	D	O		L	I	S	A	
		E	D	I	T		E	L	L	E	N			
T	H	I	R	D	D	E	G	R	E	E		T	S	K
O	A	R		W	I	N	O		D	I	J	O	N	
G	R	E	T	A		H	O	M	E	A	L	O	N	E
A	S	N	E	R		U	N	I	T		S	A	I	L
S	H	E	L	F		T	Y	R	A		A	N	A	T

55

G	A	B	E		A	D	D	U	P		Z	O	L	A
O	W	E	S		I	R	A	T	E		O	M	I	T
B	E	D	T	I	M	E	F	O	R	B	O	N	Z	O
I	D	E	A	S		S	T	P		E	L	I	A	N
			T	H	U	S		I	M	H	O			
A	R	N	E		P	A	J	A	M	A	G	A	M	E
S	A	O		S	A	G	A		E	V	I	G	A	N
C	I	V	I	C		E	B	B		E	C	O	L	I
A	M	E	L	I	E		B	I	R	D		R	E	A
P	I	L	L	O	W	T	A	L	K		M	A	S	C
			T	R	E	Y		L	O	C	O			
T	O	E	R	R		C	A	Y		I	R	I	S	H
I	D	R	E	A	M	O	F	J	E	A	N	N	I	E
E	D	N	A		R	O	T	O	S		I	F	F	Y
A	S	S	T		I	N	S	E	T		N	O	T	S

56

E	P	I	C		S	H	U	E		T	A	B	B	Y
D	O	O	R		H	E	R	R		A	C	U	R	A
A	N	N	E		O	M	N	I		B	E	B	O	P
M	Y	S	O	U	P	I	S	C	O	L	D			
			L	A	P			I	L	E		A	C	K
	A	R	E	W	E	I	N	V	I	S	I	B	L	E
C	R	O			R	O	E		O	A	K	L	E	Y
R	E	M	A	P		U	H	F		W	E	A	V	E
A	T	M	F	E	E		R	A	W			Z	E	D
W	H	E	R	E	S	O	U	R	O	R	D	E	R	
S	A	L		P	A	W		R	E	A				
		W	H	I	N	E	A	N	D	D	I	N	E	
P	A	T	I	O		S	I	L	O		D	R	U	M
A	T	O	L	L		U	R	D	U		Y	O	D	A
D	E	N	T	E		P	E	A	T		O	N	E	G

57

F	A	N	G		A	G	A	T	E		E	V	E	R
A	R	E	A		M	O	T	O	R		X	E	N	A
A	T	O	Z		O	T	E	R	I		I	R	A	N
			A	U	C	T	I	O	N	B	L	O	C	K
Y	U	M		G	O	I	N		Y	E	N	T	L	
I	N	O	I	L			I	S	T		A	S	E	
P	I	C	N	I	C	H	A	M	P	E	R			
E	S	S	O		H	O	S	E	A		U	P	A	T
			R	E	A	L	I	T	Y	C	H	E	C	K
S	A	N		L	T	D			O	R	T	H	O	
T	R	A	S	H		S	O	T	S		S	Y	S	
A	L	U	M	I	N	U	M	F	O	I	L			
M	E	S	A		A	N	I	T	A		Y	E	A	R
O	N	E	R		M	I	L	E	S		N	E	M	O
S	E	A	T		E	V	E	N	T		X	R	A	Y

58

A	L	O	O	F		S	E	M	I	S		M	O	P
L	A	R	U	E		A	B	A	S	H		A	V	E
M	I	S	T	E	R	M	A	G	O	O		S	I	P
S	C	O	W		G	E	N	A		W	A	T	T	S
			A	S	T	A		Z	A	M	B	E	Z	I
A	D	M	I	T		S	K	I	W	E	A	R		
D	I	E	T	E	D		I	N	A		A	M	O	K
O	A	T		M	I	D	T	E	R	M		I	R	E
S	L	E	D		N	E	E		E	I	S	N	E	R
		R	U	T	G	E	R	S		R	A	D	O	N
G	U	M	D	R	O	P		A	E	O	N			
E	R	A	S	E		E	A	U	X		D	R	I	P
O	B	I		M	O	N	S	T	E	R	M	A	S	H
D	A	D		O	L	D	I	E		C	A	N	E	D
E	N	S		R	E	S	T	S		A	N	T	E	S

59

D	A	D	A		F	A	T	A	L		A	M	O	K
E	G	O	S		I	N	A	N	E		L	A	V	A
C	E	P	H	A	L	O	P	O	D	S	P	R	A	Y
O	D	E		N	I	X	E	S		C	E	L	L	O
			K	W	A	I			N	O	R			
S	O	C	I	A	L	A	D	V	A	N	T	A	G	E
C	L	E	A	R		W	I	P	E		V	I	A	
A	D	D	S		P	E	E	P	S		L	I	N	T
M	I	A		P	U	R	L			M	A	S	S	E
P	E	R	S	O	N	A	L	P	R	O	N	O	U	N
			P	L	Y			H	A	R	E			
I	T	A	L	Y		B	R	A	V	O		S	I	S
D	I	S	A	P	P	E	A	R	I	N	G	I	N	K
E	L	K	S		R	A	T	O	N		O	G	R	E
M	E	S	H		E	R	A	S	E		P	H	E	W

60

R	E	A	P		E	A	R	S		G	L	A	S	S
A	X	L	E		S	T	E	P		A	U	D	I	E
Y	E	A	R		C	L	E	A	N	S	L	A	T	E
S	C	R	U	B	O	A	K		A	L	L	I	E	D
			I	R	S		E	V	A		R	D	S	
H	A	Z	M	A	T		S	W	I	M	S			
A	L	O	E	S		S	W	E	E	P	H	A	N	D
R	O	O	S		M	E	A	L	S		E	R	I	E
D	U	S	T	D	E	V	I	L		P	L	A	N	E
			A	R	D	E	N		R	I	F	L	E	D
E	S	P		A	I	R		N	E	T				
A	P	E	R	C	U		W	A	S	H	S	A	L	E
V	A	C	U	U	M	T	U	B	E		A	J	A	X
E	T	A	I	L		A	S	E	A		M	A	G	I
S	E	N	N	A		P	S	S	T		E	R	S	T

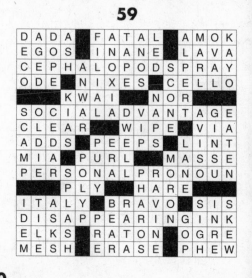

61

H	A	R	D	G		B	A	B	A	R		P	E	W
E	M	A	I	L		O	M	A	N	I		U	R	I
N	E	T	E	A	R	N	I	N	G	S		M	I	N
C	E	O		D	E	S		D	R	I	P	P	E	D
E	R	N		H	A	A	S		I	N	T	S		
		C	A	P	I	T	A	L	G	A	I	N	S	
S	E	D	A	N	S		A	N	Y		R	E	O	
O	N	E	N	D		A	R	T		F	L	O	A	T
A	Y	E		S	I	D		S	A	I	N	T	S	
P	A	P	E	R	P	R	O	F	I	T	S			
	S	O	I	L		M	I	N	T		A	R	A	
I	C	I	N	G	U	P		R	A	E		R	E	D
S	A	X		G	R	O	S	S	I	N	C	O	M	E
A	P	E		E	G	R	E	T		U	H	A	U	L
Y	E	S		D	E	K	E	S		P	E	R	S	E

62

F	C	L	E	F		S	T	R	I	P		C	A	P
A	R	E	N	A		P	I	E	C	E		H	U	H
Q	U	I	C	K	S	I	L	V	E	R		A	G	O
		L	E	A	N	T		S	K	I	R	U	N	
H	O	T	O	I	L		S	C	I		O	T	R	O
I	N	A	S	T	I	R		O	N	D	U	T	Y	
R	U	L	E		V	I	E	W		O	S	O		
E	S	E		H	A	D	A	B	I	T		P	B	S
	N	B	A		E	R	O	S		O	P	I	E	
	S	T	E	P	P	E		Y	O	N	K	E	R	S
M	I	S	T		E	M	S		B	O	A	R	D	S
E	T	C	E	T	C		T	O	A	D	Y			
N	C	O		H	A	I	R	T	R	I	G	G	E	R
S	O	U		E	N	N	U	I		C	U	R	E	D
A	M	T		A	S	S	T	S		E	Y	E	R	S

63

S	A	S	H		C	A	P	O	S		B	A	B	A
A	R	T	Y		A	N	I	M	E		E	N	O	S
R	O	O	M	S	T	O	L	E	T		A	T	O	P
A	S	O	N	E		N	O	G	O		G	I	N	S
N	E	P	A	L	I		T	A	N	G	L	E		
		L	A	N	A				R	E	L	A	X	
P	U	N	S		P	R	E	V	U	E		I	S	M
E	R	A		N	E	C	K	I	N	G		T	E	A
A	D	S		U	N	S	E	A	L		P	E	A	S
L	U	C	I	D			L	I	C	E				
	A	C	E	T	I	C		T	H	R	A	L	L	
C	A	R	E		A	V	O	W		I	G	L	O	O
A	L	F	A		N	O	V	A	S	C	O	T	I	A
S	T	A	G		G	R	E	C	O		L	A	R	D
H	O	N	E		S	Y	N	O	D		A	R	E	S

64

S	K	I	B	U	M		R	O	L	L		J	A	G
H	A	D	A	G	O		A	S	I	A		A	S	H
A	L	L	T	H	A	T	J	A	Z	Z		C	H	I
S	K	I	T		B	E	A	K		E	W	O	K	
T	A	N	Y	A		C	H	A	R		A	B	E	D
A	N	G		L	A	H		N	E	W	L	I	N	E
			S	E	I	N	E		T	A	R	T	A	N
A	L	E	X	R	O	D	R	I	G	U	E	Z		
B	L	A	R	E	D		T	U	N	E	S			
M	C	G	U	I	R	E		P	A	R		S	F	C
W	A	R	M		Y	U	M	A		S	L	Y	E	R
	T	A	S	K		R	O	U	T		E	Z	R	A
U	R	N		A	P	O	L	L	O	S	O	Y	U	Z
Z	A	G		T	Y	P	E		J	I	N	G	L	E
I	Z	E		E	X	E	S		O	B	E	Y	E	D

65

G	I	B	E		Z	A	G	S			A	L	L	I
O	N	E	A		A	G	A	I	N		C	O	A	L
O	L	E	S		N	O	R	M	A		T	A	N	K
G	E	N	T	L	E	O	N	M	Y	M	I	N	D	
L	A	I	L	A		D	I	S	S	E	V	E	R	
I	G	N	A	T	Z				A	I	R	Y		
N	U	T		O	B	T	A	I	N	S				
G	E	O	R	G	I	A	O	N	M	Y	M	I	N	D
	A	R	C	A	D	I	A			N	O	W		
	A	B	I	E			M	I	N	I	M	I		
V	O	L	T	A	I	R	E		C	U	T	I	N	
A	L	W	A	Y	S	O	N	M	Y	M	I	N	D	
P	L	E	A		E	L	U	D	E		B	A	L	L
R	O	R	Y		S	E	T	O	N		E	T	T	E
E	N	O	S		S	E	W	S		R	E	E	D	

66

```
S P A M   M A C S   S E G A R
T A D A   A L A W   I R E N E
O N U S   D O M E   C I T G O
W E L C O M E P A C K E T
E L T O R O   R A D   O P S
      T E N N I S R A C K E T
L B J   S E E P   Y E N T L
I O U S   Y E A S T   L O R E
B R I A R   N O A H   W O O
Y E L L O W J A C K E T
A S L   A H A   E R A S E S
    I N C O M E B R A C K E T
C O A C H   M I L O   T O R I
A U R A E   E R O O   I S I N
M I D A S   D E B T   C H E T
```

67

```
C I R C   M E O W S   E D A M
A L O U   A T E A M   L E G O
D E L T A F O R C E   P L U S
S A L A M I   S A R A L E E
      R E A L M (M)   R A S A
M O D U S   (A G O)   C O R G I
O N E G   (I M M U N E)   E I N
V A L   (D R E)   T A (D)   E N S
I I I   (Y E N T A S)   P S S T
E R N I E   (T E T)   S O E U R
    Q T R S   (A E S O P)
H A U L S I N   U P S A L A
A B E L   D E L I G H T F U L
L E N D   E R I C A   A R N E
O T T O   D O V E R   R O T S
```

68

```
T A C K   S P A S M   L I A M
A L A I   I G L O O   A N C E
C A R D I N A L N U M B E R S
O N E N D   S N O O Z E S
    A L O E S   D U H
R E D P E P P E R   S E T U P
I L A   T I D E   E M O T E
F I R S T   L A V   D E B I T
L A T T E   O L E O   A C E
E S S E X   G I A N T S T A R
    A M P   A L E U T
A L A M E I N   F E R A L
M E T E X P E C T A T I O N S
I G O R   E V I A N   N O T A
D O N S   R E A D Y   S K I T
```

69

```
A M I N   T A M P A   A S P S
C A N T   A L I A S   S A L E
H I G H C H U R C H   S P I N
E N O   A I M   D U P E D
D E T E C T   S P E E C H
    W H I C H I S W H I C H
T H R E E   H E N S   R O O
B O O S T   A A A   I D E A L
A B A   M I T T   N A S T Y
R O S H H A S H A N A H
    T O U P E E   I S L A N D
A R B O R   A C E   C O O
D E E P   F O U R H C L U B S
O P E L   C A R N E   A T E E
S O F A   C R I E S   G E L S
```

70

```
I D E A L   B A A   A G O G
C I R R I   U R N S   C E D E
B L A C K S M I T H   I T E M
M A S S E U R   S E E D S
S T E   B A R   L I M I T
    E D E L   P E T T Y C A S H
      M I T   C O O S   R I O
    U N I T E D A R T I S T S
F D A   H A I R   E A T
Y O U N G L O V E   N A R C
I N T O O   E A N   E L I
    I O W A S   R O O S T E D
B A L D   B R O W N S T O N E
A Z U L   S A R A   L O R C A
N O S E   S A X   O A T H S
```

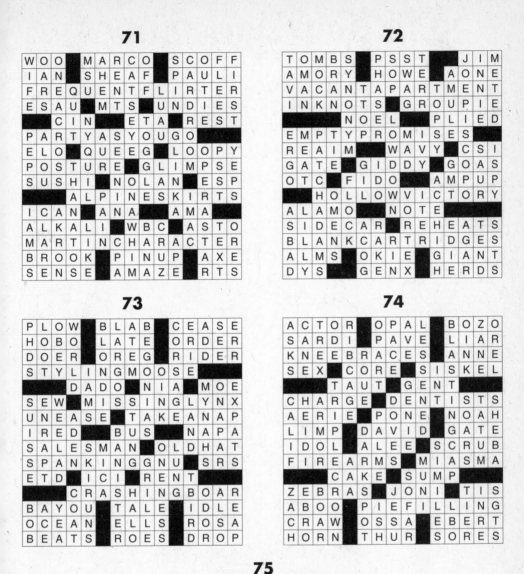

71

```
W O O   M A R C O   S C O F F
I A N   S H E A F   P A U L I
F R E Q U E N T F L I R T E R
E S A U   M T S   U N D I E S
    C I N     E T A   R E S T
P A R T Y A S Y O U G O
E L O   Q U E E G   L O O P Y
P O S T U R E   G L I M P S E
S U S H I   N O L A N   E S P
    A L P I N E S K I R T S
I C A N   A N A   A M A
A L K A L I   W B C   A S T O
M A R T I N C H A R A C T E R
B R O O K   P I N U P   A X E
S E N S E   A M A Z E   R T S
```

72

```
T O M B S   P S S T     J I M
A M O R Y   H O W E   A O N E
V A C A N T A P A R T M E N T
I N K N O T S   G R O U P I E
      N O E L   P L I E D
E M P T Y P R O M I S E S
R E A I M   W A V Y   C S I
G A T E   G I D D Y   G O A S
O T C   F I D O   A M P U P
  H O L L O W V I C T O R Y
A L A M O   N O T E
S I D E C A R   R E H E A T S
B L A N K C A R T R I D G E S
A L M S   O K I E   G I A N T
D Y S   G E N X   H E R D S
```

73

```
P L O W   B L A B   C E A S E
H O B O   L A T E   O R D E R
D O E R   O R E G   R I D E R
S T Y L I N G M O O S E
    D A D O   N I A   M O E
S E W   M I S S I N G L Y N X
U N E A S E   T A K E A N A P
I R E D   B U S   N A P A
S A L E S M A N   O L D H A T
S P A N K I N G G N U   S R S
E T D   I C I   R E N T
    C R A S H I N G B O A R
B A Y O U   T A L E   I D L E
O C E A N   E L L S   R O S A
B E A T S   R O E S   D R O P
```

74

```
A C T O R   O P A L   B O Z O
S A R D I   P A V E   L I A R
K N E E B R A C E S   A N N E
S E X   C O R E   S I S K E L
    T A U T   G E N T
C H A R G E   D E N T I S T S
A E R I E   P O N E   N O A H
L I M P   D A V I D   G A T E
I D O L   A L E E   S C R U B
F I R E A R M S   M I A S M A
    C A K E   S U M P
Z E B R A S   J O N I   T I S
A B O O   P I E F I L L I N G
C R A W   O S S A   E B E R T
H O R N   T H U R   S O R E S
```

75

```
A D A M   C R O W D   T O T E
S I D E   L E M O N   A V I S
S C E N E O F A N A C C E N T
T E N   U S E R   A O R T A
    B R E R   P E R M
R E P R O S   S A L T A W A Y
A R I A   M E R L E   A L I
C O N T I N E N T A L D I V E
E D U   N E E D Y   E V I L
D E P O S I T S   D E F E N D
    B A N S   R E L Y
P R E E N   N I N E   T H E
R A P R E S P O N S E T E A M
O R E O   A R I S E   A L I I
P E E N   S E D E R   P E R L
```